The $\mathcal{A}$*rt of*

the **Lathe**

The Art of the Lathe
Award Winning Designs

Patrick Spielman

Sterling Publishing Co., Inc. New York

A Sterling/Chapelle Book

For Chapelle Limited

Owner: Jo Packham

Editorial: Leslie Ridenour and Cindy Stoeckl

Staff: Malissa Boatwright, Sara Casperson, Rebecca Christensen, Amber Hansen, Holly Hollingsworth, Susan Jorgensen, Susan Laws, Amanda McPeck, Barbara Milburn, Pat Pearson, Cindy Rooks, Ryanne Webster and Nancy Whitley

Photographers: Kevin Dilley for Hazen Photography, Mark Johnsen for Moonlight Photography, and Patrick Spielman

Photo Stylist: Susan Laws

Technical Drawings: Roxanne LeMoine and Lorna Johnson

Library of Congress Cataloging-in-Publication Data

Spielman, Patrick E.
      The art of the lathe : award winning designs / Patrick Spielman.
            p.   cm.
      "A Sterling/Chapelle book."
      Includes index.
      ISBN 0-8069-4272-X
      1. Turning. 2. Lathes. 3. Woodworkers—United States. I. Title.
      TT201.S72 1996
      684'.083—dc20   95-48770
                                                                        CIP

10 9 8 7 6 5 4 3

A Sterling/Chapelle Book

Published by Sterling Publishing Company, Inc.
387 Park Avenue South, New York, N.Y. 10016
© 1996 by Patrick Spielman and Chapelle Ltd.
Distributed in Canada by Sterling Publishing
ᶜ/ₒ Canadian Manda Group, One Atlantic Avenue, Suite 105
Toronto, Ontario, Canada M6K 3E7
Distributed in Great Britain and Europe by Cassell PLC
Wellington House, 125 Strand, London WC2R 0BB, England
Distributed in Australia by Capricorn Link (Australia) Pty Ltd.
P.O. Box 6651, Baulkham Hills, Business Centre, NSW 2153, Australia
Printed in Hong Kong
All Rights Reserved

Sterling ISBN 0-8069-4272-X

On Cover: Bud Latven's Prairie Island, Brazilian purpleheart, African ebony and avonite, 9½" H x 16" DIA (Fleur Bresler private collection)

On Page 2: Giles Gilson's Vase with lid and necklace (orange), exotic woods, lacquered wood, aluminum and stainless steel, 32" H x 16" DIA (Singer collection)

On Page 3: Hugh McKay's Splash, black myrtle and soapstone, 4" H x 11" x 11"

Every effort has been made to ensure that all of the information in this book is accurate. However, due to differing conditions, tools, and individual skills, the publisher cannot be responsible for any injuries, losses, and/or other damages which may result from the use of the information in this book.

If you have any questions or comments or would like information about any specialty products featured in this book, please contact:

Chapelle Ltd., Inc.
PO Box 9252
Ogden, UT 84409

Phone: (801) 621-2777, FAX: (801) 621-2788

Contents

Chapter 1

A Visual Celebration

In this book I seek to initiate a type of forum to present some comprehensive production techniques which may not be commonplace, to set the spotlight on the concepts and creations of some of today's most exciting woodturning artists, and to stimulate you, the turner, to develop new ideas for using this tool called the lathe. All turners have their own specific style, their own preference for lathes, their own special grinds on their own tools and chisels, and their own unique techniques for working their choice of materials. There are many different approaches to completing singular turning tasks. For example, a turner may use several different tools, applying each to a different piece of wood in a different manner and still end up with the same bead.

The aim of *The Art of the Lathe* is that of an inspiration book— a visual celebration of the state of the art of woodturning. The means to this end is found in the artistic photographs of original award-winning lathe-produced pieces created by many of the world's most recognized and accomplished woodturners. It is an enormous thrill and privilege to present and showcase this varied collection of exceptional turnings.

The exhibit of various turnings in this book offers an interchange of styles and ideas that is certain to cultivate and inspire the creative capabilities of all who venture through these pages. Evidenced by the collection of pieces displayed, turning is a woodworking area that is very fertile ground for the

Hollow Vase by Bob Chapman

creative craftsperson who has an open mind. Just as these artistic turners have logged long hours in practicing skills, pioneering techniques with new materials and tooling, and thereby elevating this craft to an art form, so too may your directions, execution and expressive abilities expand. I hope you will fuse your own materials, techniques, and tooling capabilities with the ideas presented, subsequently enriching and increasing your overall abilities and execution. Your turning scope and imagination will multiply many fold from studying the fine pieces offered here and becoming familiar with the featured artists' background, interests and directions. Most of these artists enjoy a nonconforming, unrestricted freedom of expression. Even the most experienced woodturners can find value here.

Using the lathe, sculptural and utilitarian objects can be created with comparative ease in a relatively short time. Therein lies the excitement and appeal of woodturning. The lathe permits the working of a piece of wood from a tree that is grown nearby into a completely finished three-dimensional product. Expansive shop space and other supporting, expensive woodworking equipment, such as planers and saws are not necessary.

Although turning wood is a machine operation, it is still an experience of the mind, the hand, and the eye coordinated with full-body movements. One prominent turner refers to the lathe as an efficient carving tool. It is fairly easy to learn the basics of the lathe and to enjoy using it in a relatively short period of time. However, developing skill and proficiency requires much practice and experimentation.

Just as it is important to view and study the works of today's great turners, it is also recommended to observe all cylindrical art forms, including turned antiques from other eras as well as works from other cultures and other lands. The study of glass, pottery, and metals is essential to the overall development of individual tastes and provides a rich storehouse of turning expressions. Professional, experienced and dedicated woodturning artists have an unlimited mental warehouse of shapes and forms that can be adapted to a specific turned object or a certain mass of raw wood.

For the less experienced, the assistance of drawing-board designs are helpful in arriving at desirable forms. Thus, a number of prepared drawings and patterns for practice turning objects have been included. These, combined with numerous illustrations of several design elements for practicing various forms, will especially help the beginner. Also included are some noteworthy discussions of selected topics and tips to acquaint those who are less experienced with some new and helpful material not commonly addressed in other books.

Learning to Turn

Outside of full-time enrollment in a public or private school specializing in woodworking or woodturning, there are many ways for beginners to learn and for amateurs to improve their present level of turning skills. Assuming that an excellent instructor is available to you, the following is a list, in descending order, of courses of action recommended to take:

1. A personal tutor in your shop using your tools and equipment.

2. Personal tutor, one-on-one, in the tutor's shop.

3. Group hands-on experience in tutor's shop.

4. Attending seminars and symposia with live demonstrations by experts.

5. Viewing videos (and reviewing frequently) of demonstrations and instruction by experts.

6. Reading books, magazines and various manufacturer's catalogues.

7. Trial-and-error experimentation on your own.

Regardless of which avenue or any combination of opportunities is pursued, much practice is still necessary. There are no magic shortcuts to advancing from novice to professional craftsperson or to production turner or woodturning artist.

Finding an instructor or instructional program that is best for your personal situation could prove to be a dilemma. However, there are several organizations and publications available. There may even be a local turning club in your area. If not, consider starting a club. Forming a local club enables your group to bring instructors to your locality—a task that is difficult to afford or accomplish as an individual.

The benefits of belonging to a national organization dedicated to woodturning are many. There are national turning associations in most countries (Fig. 1-1). The American Association of Woodturners is always seeking new members. They now number more than 5,000 and have over 60 local affiliated clubs in many states. This organization has a nine-member volunteer board of directors, an administrator and a journal editor. Members receive the Association's excellent ideas- and news-filled quarterly journal, *American Woodturner,* and an annual resource directory. This inclusive publication provides listings of local chapters, of woodturning instructors, and of fellow turners state by state. It also chronicles books, videos and other resources. Membership is effective per calendar year and general dues are extremely reasonable. Their office is located in Shoreview, Minnesota.

The Wood Turning Center is another nonprofit organization with international presence. Based in Philadelphia, it has been dedicated to the growth, encouragement and enhancement of the lathe-turning field since 1976. The Center provides a vital forum for artists and craftspeople who create lathe-turned objects. The Center's publication is *Turning Points* (Fig. 1-1). Turners are encouraged to push their creative expression and technical capabilities by participating in the Center's popular *Challenge* exhibits and other forums that recognize and promote excellence in the field.

Fig. 1-1   Excellent periodicals of interest to serious woodturners. *Woodturning Magazine* from England is published 10 times per year. *Turning Points* is a newsletter from the Wood Turning Center. *American Woodturner* is published quarterly by the American Association of Woodturners.

By purposefully building its museum collections and in its sponsorship of local and traveling exhibits, the Center promotes turning, and in the process, exposes museum professionals, collectors and the public to the best in the craft. The Wood Turning Center also plays an important role in preserving and interpreting the history of turning. The Center's resources are unique in the scope of their documentation of turning, including historical information, slides, videos and records on individual artists and their work. The Center is committed to promoting increased historical and critical interest in the field through programs such as its World Turning Conference, and to making its extensive resources accessible to artists, scholars, collectors and others.

Membership in the Wood Turning Center and a subscription to *Turning Points* are available to all who practice lathe-turning or share an interest in the craft. The office is located in Philadelphia, Pennsylvania.

Another magazine devoted to lathe-turned pieces is *Woodturning* (Fig. 1-1). It is a full color 10-issue per year British publication produced by the Guild of Master Craftsmen. This is an excellent magazine with regular features that include projects, new technology and techniques, biographical sketches of turners from around the world, tips, book and video reviews, information about turning classes and instructors, manufacturers' advertisements and numerous other tidbits of interest to woodturners. To acquire this publication, contact the Guild of Master Craftsmen, East Sussex, England.

Brief History

Turning is one of the only woodworking processes that combines hand-tool skills with machine power. It is the only woodworking process by which the material is rotated or moved under power as a more or less fixed, hand-controlled cutting tool is applied to the spinning wood. From that point of view, woodturning has remained unchanged since its inception.

Evolution of Turning Lathes

The bow lathe (Fig. 1-2) is the first woodworking machine recorded in history. It is believed to have been invented in about 740 B.C. in Egypt. The bow lathe supported the work between two pointed pieces of wood. The bow string made one loop around the workpiece. While the woodturner moved the bow forward and backward with one hand, the work rotated alternately in opposite directions. The cutting tool was applied to the work only while it rotated toward the operator.

The spring-pole lathe (Fig. 1-3) was also used by the ancient Egyptians. This type of lathe operated on the same principle as the bow lathe, except that the operator was free to use both hands to control the cutting tool. A rope was fastened to the end of either a tree branch, a young sapling, or if indoors, a spring pole fastened to the ceiling. The rope extended downward, made one turn around the work-piece, and the lower end was tied into a loop to serve as a "foot treadle." When the woodturner pressed down on the treadle, the rope rotated the work and sprung the tree branch. When the operator released his foot pressure,

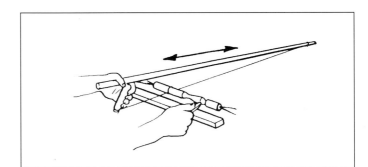

Fig. 1-2   The bow lathe was used in Egypt as far back as 740 B.C.

8

Fig. 1-3 The pole lathe was used until the 18th century. It is still used today in some remote parts of the world.

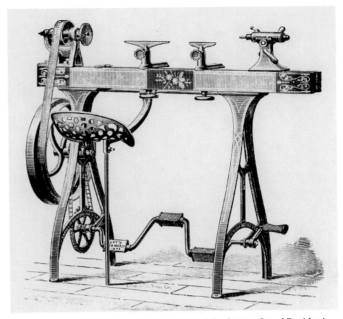

Fig. 1-4 This 12" lathe produced by W.F. & John Barnes Co. of Rockford, Illinois sold for $40 at the turn of the century. Known as the No. 3 velocipede foot-powered lathe, it featured work speeds varying upwards to 1000 and 2000 rpm. All parts were made of iron and steel, except the bed, which was made of wood. Net weight was 230 pounds.

the tree branch or spring pole pulled the rope up again and reversed the rotation of the workpiece. Like the operation of the bow lathe, the cutting tool was applied to the work only when the rotation was toward the operator, or, in other words, against the cutting tool.

The pole lathe was used for many centuries without much improvement. In some parts of the world, it was used until the eighteenth century. The early lathes were made of wood, except for the two centers which supported the ends of the work. These were made of iron, as were the cutting tools themselves. In around A.D. 1200, man conceived the crankshaft and the idea of transmitting rotary power through belts looped over wheels. This power source was adapted to the lathe. The drive wheel was powered by a foot treadle connected to a crankshaft. A belt connected the drive wheel to a spindle pulley. This drive mechanism produced a continuous rotary movement of the workpiece. A popular turn-of-the-century foot-powered lathe of the pre-electric power machine era is shown in Fig. 1-4.

Turning Tools (Chisels and Gouges)

The general design and function of lathe tools really haven't changed a great deal since early times (Fig. 1-5). The five basic tools still include either shear cutting or scraping devices. However, recently some

important and innovative refinements in tooling have occurred. There are some changes in design configurations, especially in profiles and grinding angles or bevels and also in metal technology. The latter has produced harder materials and tools with edges that stay sharp longer.

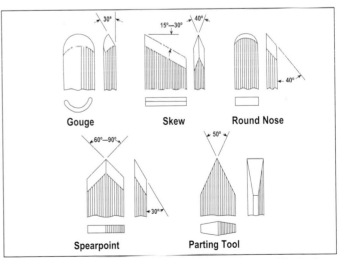

Fig. 1-5 Profiles and cross-sectional shapes of a classic set of five basic turning chisels and scrapers. These tools remained essentially unchanged in design until the last 20 years. Some are still used as is or in modified grinds by turners today.

9

Chapter 2

The Lathe

Lathes

As one expert puts it, "All lathes are not created equal," and what is produced or made on one lathe is not necessarily possible on another. So, what makes a good lathe? Rigidity and stiffness that minimize vibration are important features for large and heavy work. Since many turners are taking advantage of the costs and availability benefits associated with turning locally available green or wet wood, a well-built sturdy lathe is essential. Such a lathe must be capable of safely rotating the heavy and often initially out of balance chunks of wood especially during the early stages of the turning process.

Lathes come in floor-model or bench-top versions, and are of various work-size capacities, and with numerous differences in structural and overall design features. The size of all lathes is designated by the maximum diameter of work that may be swung over the bed and the maximum length of stock that may be held between the two centers. The bed on larger-model lathes is made of heavy cast iron, and lighter-duty lathes generally have tubular steel construction.

To make a general recommendation about which lathe to buy or which is best is like telling someone what kind of car to own or how much to pay for a new suit. Only the potential user can make this judgment. Space here doesn't permit lengthy discussions about lathes in general—or in particular for that matter. Much of this information is available in books and can be gleaned from current manufacturers' catalogs.

When planning the purchase of a lathe, it may be beneficial to seek out older, used lathes. I purchased an old 14" Oliver, variable-speed,

Fig. 2-1   My Oliver lathe was purchased used at much less than new price. This lathe has remained unchanged in its basic design for about 60 years.

Fig. 2-2   The Union Graduate lathes have been a favorite of English turners for years. They have an outboard capacity of 18" in diameter, a 6" center height and a choice of 30, 42, and 54 inches between centers. *Photo courtesy of Graduate Lathe Company Ltd.*

1-HP lathe (Fig. 2-1) from a school that was making cutbacks in its woodworking program. The lathe weighs approximately 700 pounds and is of all cast iron construction. If it were ordered new today, the cost would be around $12,000. It is important to take a look at all the lathes available, including those from other countries. Two popular heavy-duty lathes imported to the United States are shown in Figs. 2-2 and 2-3. Just a few other heavier lathes to consider are Conover, Delta (Fig. 2-4), Enlon, General, Hegner, Jet, Mini-Max, Myford, Powermatic, Record, Vega, Woodtech and Woodfast.

A popular bench-top "starter" lathe is the 12" Delta, shown in Fig. 2-5. Other small, lightweight but fun lathes are shown in Figs. 2-6 and 2-7. The Klein lathe (Fig. 2-7) weighs only about 10 pounds, but it's not a toy. It was developed especially for creating high-quality turned miniatures and small project work such as pens, bottle stoppers and so on. It has many optional accessories available with features that are comparable to metal lathes, including a threading jig. This jig permits making not only threaded dowels of all sizes up to 5" in diameter, but also cylindrical boxes with threaded lids.

Fig. 2-4   Delta's newest heavy-duty lathe is this 1½-HP, 16" model that weighs 410 pounds with five speeds ranging between 350 and 3,000 rpm with a V-belt drive. Optional outboard bowl attachment permits turning bowls up to 32" in diameter. It has a 40" spindle length turning capacity.

Fig. 2-3   The Australian-made 1½ HP Woodfast lathes are available in 12-, 16-, and 20-inch swings and in bed lengths from just 16" between centers or to their long bed which is about 30" between centers. It can be ordered with a variable-speed or in five-speed belted drive models. Net weight ranges from 385 to 520 pounds. These very popular lathes cost between slightly more than $2,000 to around $2,600. They are imported into the United States by Craft Supplies USA of Provo, Utah. *Photo courtesy of Craft Supplies USA.*

Fig. 2-5   Delta's 12" variable-speed, bench-top lathe mounted on a shop-made turning bench. Note the use of sandbags to give added weight and rigidity. This lathe will handle stock 36" between centers. It features a pivoting headstock permitting outboard turnings up to 16" in diameter. Total weight is 125 pounds without bench and sandbags.

Fig. 2-6   The RYOBI 6¼" mini-lathe is a good starter lathe, and its small size makes it easily portable. It has a direct-drive 2½-amp motor in headstock with a variable-speed control range from 500 to 2,500 rpm. Its capacity between centers is 18", and the entire lathe weighs just 30 pounds.

Fig. 2-7   The Klein miniature lathe has a 5" swing and is 12" between centers. Klein Design of Renton, Washington, also makes three- or four-jaw chucks, small turning tools, a threading jig, an indexing plate, drill chucks and collet sets to accompany this lathe. It's driven by a ⅙ or ¼ HP motor that is not standard but available as an option. *Photo courtesy of Bonnie Klein.*

Some Desirable Lathe Features & Options

1. A No. 2 morse taper headstock spindle accommodates most accessories such as a Jacob's drill chuck.

2. A live tailstock cup center that rotates with the workpiece.

3. A spindle lock makes removing faceplates easy and fast.

4. A quick lock cam or lever clamps on the tool rest and tailstock.

5. A hollow tailstock spindle with a hollow cup center for deep hole end drilling of spindle work.

6. A variable-speed drive slow enough for large, rough turnings.

7. A large and comfortable outboard hand wheel and faceplate that permits hand pressure to stop lathe rotation after power is shut off.

8. Using common headstock spindle size and threads so that available accessories such as three- or four-jaw and screw chucks will fit (Figs. 4-30 to 4-32 on page 32).

9. If you do fluting and reeding of spindle work for faceplate division work, consider a unit with a spindle-indexing lock mechanism (Figs. 4-35 to 4-37 on pages 33-34).

10. If you intend to do a lot of faceplate work, consider a short-bed lathe and one with easily removable and replaceable tailstock assembly so that you avoid hitting your elbow on the tailstock center.

Lathe Tips

1. Smooth and polish the top edge of the tool rest, use a flat mill file and apply paste wax. File off sharp edges or corners of turning tools, such as skews and parting tools that might nick the tool rest (Fig. 2-8).

2. Do not polish and wax the ways of the lathe. Tailstock and tool rest support will slip.

3. Consider using an auxiliary foot switch or wire a remote switch that is conveniently close to your frequent body position.

4. Light your work area sufficiently.

5. Add weight (such as sand bags) and bench or stand stiffening measures to reduce vibration (Fig. 2-5).

6. Bolt floor-model lathes to the floor.

7. Block or fix lathe at optimum working height—normally with lathe centers at elbow height.

Fig. 2-8   Tip: Smooth and polish the top edge of the tool rest.

Chapter **3**

Tools & Sharpening Today

The tools available today for shaping lathe-rotated wood encompass a vast array of styles and shapes in various sizes (Fig. 3-1). Turning tools are made of different metal compositions with various handle designs in short to long lengths with some incorporating revolutionary new design configurations. Still, the best tool choice is a matter of individual preference, the nature of the work at hand, and the turner's skill level.

In woodturning you will find a greater range of angles and bevels on tools used for cutting than any other area of woodworking. Bevels range from as blunt as 85 degrees to as acute as 20 degrees. Each special grind results in different cutting actions, and each individual tool needs to be applied to the wood correctly to achieve the optimum benefit (Fig. 3-2).

All the choices and special adaptations recommended by different experts and manufacturers often cloud the basic rules of selection and use. Very skilled turners can do many things with very few tools. For example, a skilled artist with a gouge (Fig. 3-2) can form beads on spindle work, turn end grain, form the inside and outside of bowls or vessels, and decorate their surfaces with beads or cove cuts. On the other hand, very specialized single-purpose tools, such as one designed for making only a particular size of bead or a similar specialty tool designed exclusively for forming captive rings around spindles, are also available for purchase.

Three keys to turning success are 1) proper tool selection, 2) skillful sharpening, and 3) capable tool manipulation or tool-use techniques. Size and rigidity of the lathe, the kind, size and condition of the material (wet, dry, hard or soft), end grain or side grain, and the tooling available all play a role in how to approach a specific turning. However, the focus here is an overview of the tools available today and a glimpse of some of the newer innovations in turning tools and techniques.

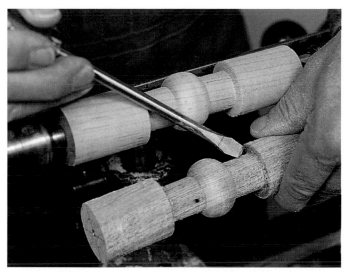

Fig. 3-1   Turned hardwood (black cherry) in the lathe compared to a softer wood (butternut). Both were formed with the unaltered screw driver shown Note the rough, torn fibers on the surfaces and shoulder of the butternut.

Fig. 3-2   The other extremes are these examples of difficult to turn woods (Douglas fir and lauan) with the cut surfaces sheared clean with a sharp gouge. This demonstrates the fact that if the end grains on these species can be cut this cleanly, other hardwoods of almost any species will be easy to turn without any torn fibers.

Until the late 1950s most turning tools were made of high-carbon steels. Then high-speed tool steel appeared, showing much promise and offering as much as six times longer sharpness between sharpenings. For further improvement, the metallurgical challenge was to produce a hard edge-holding material without it becoming dangerously too brittle.

Today, one manufacturer, Glaser Engineering of Playa del Rey, California, offers their Hi-Tech turning tools (Fig. 3-3). They are made of an A-11-type tool steel with 10 percent vanadium. This manufacturer claims their edge will stay sharp four times longer than those made of other high-speed tool materials. The perfect tool that never needs sharpening is yet to be developed, but, as demonstrated, new technology is moving closer to this goal.

Scrapers

Fig. 3-4 shows a variety of scraping tools. Scrapers should have blunt bevels of around 45 to 60 degrees (as these bevels approach 90 degrees, the scraper is more apt to dig into the turning). They are usually used direct from the grinder without honing or removing the resulting burr, which permits taking light finishing cuts on bowls and similar projects. Scrapers are seldom used on spindle work between centers. Thick and heavy high-speed steel scrapers are usually preferred for faceplate work because they minimize vibration.

Gouges

Typically there are three basic kinds of gouges, the roughing gouge, the spindle gouge and the bowl gouge (Figs. 3-5 and 3-6). One popular gouge for bowls and large-diameter spindle work is a ½" or 9/16" deep-fluted gouge, shown in Figs. 3-7 to 3-9. Most turning experts experiment and prefer their own special grinds on their gouges, obtaining specific results in their turning specialty. Consequently, you will find many versions of gouges. See Figs. 3-7 through 3-10. Some bowl and vessel turners work wet wood to very thin wall thicknesses. They seek fine, delicate but controlled shearing cuts. This technique practically eliminates sanding, which doesn't always cut to uniform depth due to variation of the grain and its orientation.

Skews

Skews (Fig. 3-11 on page 16) look like double-bevel chisels that are mainly used for spindle work.

Fig. 3-3   The Glaser Hi-Tech turning tools include various gouges, scrapers, skews, and parting tools.

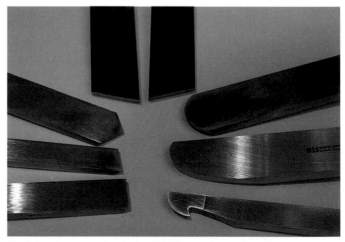

Fig. 3-4   Some scraping tools with different edge configurations.

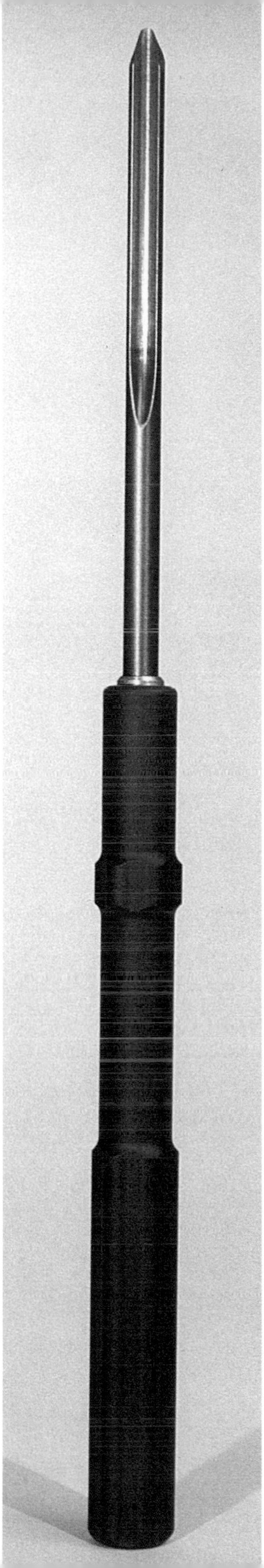

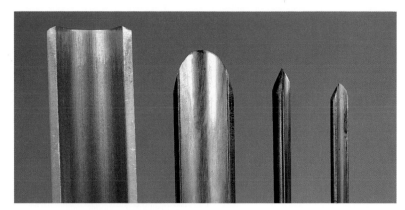

Fig. 3-7 The Glaser Hi-Tech ½"-deep gouge. This tool features A-11 tool steel with 10 percent vanadium and 2 percent carbon for high wear resistance. The unique easy-grip handle is hollow, extruded aluminum with heavy lead shot fill to dampen vibration.

Fig. 3-5 Gouges. Left to right: large roughing gouge, three spindle gouges in different sizes and views. (Note the differences of bevel angles.)

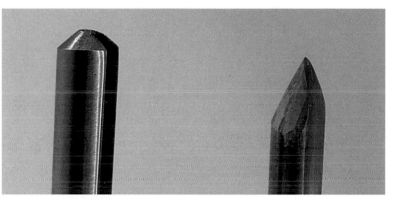

Fig. 3-6 A typical deep-flute bowl gouge at the left compared to a typical spindle gouge.

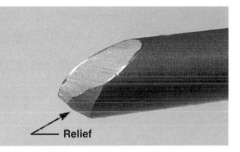

Relief

Fig. 3-8 A relief grind of the Glaser deep-flute gouge provides clearance when turning an inside radius.

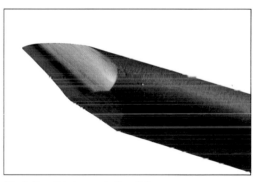

Fig. 3-10 Grind on a shallow-flute gouge.

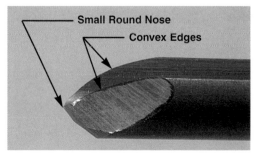

Small Round Nose

Convex Edges

Fig. 3-9 Another view of the Glaser deep-flute gouge.

15

Besides forming beads and large-radius convex shapes, their major function is to make straight and taper cuts. As with most tools, skews come in a variety of sizes and have various cross-sectional shapes including round and oval shapes (not pictured). As with any cutting tool, the sharper the skew the better. The skew seems to be the most difficult tool to master, but placed in the hands of a proficient spindle turner, it is very much like the brush in the hand of an accomplished portrait artist.

Fig. 3-11   Skews. Left to right: a typical skew, the Raffan skew with its slightly curved cutting edge, the roll-edge skew with rounded edges, a full round skew, and a regular skew with a "Stabilax" attachment. The latter two claim to roll more smoothly over the tool rest for better control and thus are generally more "user friendly."

Parting Tools

Parting tools (Fig. 3-12) are used to part off the turning from the waste, establish various sizing diameters, and cut small flat areas not accessible with other tools. Parting tools have applications in both spindle and faceplate work. Parting tools have various cross-sectional shapes that are designed to minimize side friction, with the diamond style being probably the most popular. Some experts grind or make their own with side clearance to minimize friction and heat buildup when making

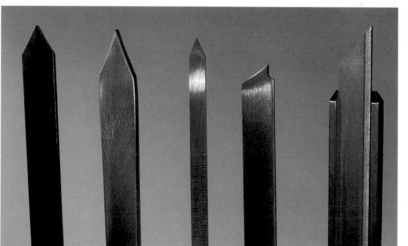

Fig. 3-12   Parting tools. Left to right: a typical diamond cross-sectional shape, large and small flat tools, Kip Christensen's modified version and at the far right is the Beech Street Tool Work's thin kerf, T-shaped, and adjustable length blade—a new innovation in parting tool design.

Fig. 3-13   The Beech Street Tool Works parting tool.

fairly deep cuts. One radically different design comes from Beech Street Tool Works of Los Angeles, California. This unique parting tool (Figs. 3-13 to 3-15) features a thin $\frac{1}{16}$" kerf cut with a "T"-shaped blade adjustable in a sturdy holder. Note the close-up photo and cross-sectional drawing. The holder can be adjusted to act as a depth-of-cut stop when sizing diameters on duplicate turnings. However, the adjustment must be made with an Allen wrench and set screws, which may be too time-consuming for production work.

Some turnings require the use of specialty turning tools. There are many interesting turning tools of unusual design and/or function.

Ring Tools

Ring tools (Fig. 3-16) are designed primarily for cutting end grains, such as when deep-hollowing the insides of goblets, vases and similar work. When sharp and cutting properly, they produce excellent cuts. However, shearing off end grain always presents problems and a "catch" can severely damage or ruin the piece.

Chatter Tools

Chatter tools (Figs. 3-17 and 3-18 on page 18) create unusual decorative patterns by the action of a flexible blade that vibrates against the rotating wood. Various patterns are achieved by changing the lathe speed, the length of cutter, the shape of the cutting edge, the angle to the work, and so on. Note that the blade length is adjustable by a thumbscrew. Chatter work is best done on hard, dense woods and particularly end grain.

Tools with Interchangeable Tips

Robert Sorby Tools of Sheffield, England, are leaders in offering multiple-tip, multipurpose tools and/or "systems" that utilize interchangeable components (Figs. 3-19 to 3-28 on pages 19 through 21). These are

Fig. 3-14   A close-up of the $\frac{1}{16}$" x $\frac{1}{2}$" x 4" blade and blade holder.

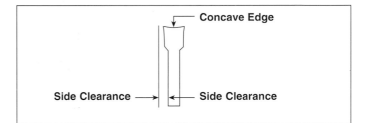

Fig. 3-15   Cross-sectional shape and grinding features of the Beech Street Tool Work's unusual "parting/sizing" tool.

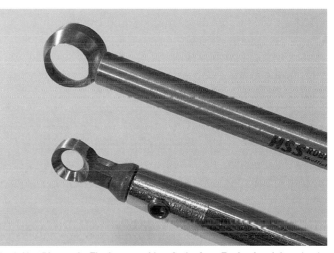

Fig. 3-16   Ring tools. The larger tool is a Sorby from England and the other is the "Termite" multiple-tip ring tool made in Canada, but available from Packard Woodworks of Tryon, North Carolina. The Termite has $\frac{5}{16}$"- and $\frac{7}{16}$"-diameter interchangeable cutters.

scrapers or parting tool cutting configurations of differently shaped cutting edges. This concept offers the user many options and adjustable tool positions, but it does not have the same convenience of quickly switching to separate, dedicated tools. Changing cutters takes some time, and sharpening some of the small cutters presents some interesting holding problems at the grinder. The simplest holding method is to mount the cutters upside down on the tool holder and present it to the grinding wheel with the bevel up to gain access to it. For shear scraper blades, the manufacturer recommends a bevel angle of 60 degrees for softwoods and 70 to 80 or 90 degrees for hardwoods (impossible for regular scraping). Generally, they can be used with the burr, but honing with a 90-degree bevel improves the standard of surface (finish) significantly.

Sharpening

Most expert turners have their own techniques and individual theories about tool sharpening, and I don't intend to inject another method. I do, however, suggest that you find a fast and simple technique, because even modern turning tools must be sharpened more often than one may suppose. In fact, some turners keep the grinder right next to the lathe (Fig. 3-29 on page 21).

Remember not to "blue," or overheat the edges of the tools made of carbon-tool steels. They should be cooled in water frequently during the grinding process. However, high-speed steel is more forgiving and slightly bluing the edge will have a minimal effect on the tool's ability to cut. Most experts agree that an aluminum oxide wheel of 60 or 80 grit is generally the best grinding medium to use. Thus, it is recommended to replace the stock silicon carbide wheels that come as standard equipment with the grinder. It's also generally agreed that a slow-speed grinder, such as 1,725, rpm is much better for sharpening turning tools than the standard 3,450 rpm version.

Although sharpening skews and gouges on the side of the wheel may seem easier because the bevel is visible throughout the grinding process (Fig. 3-30 on page 21), this practice should be kept at a minimum. This system does not produce a hollow grind, which best lends itself to honing with regular or diamond stones, and it is also dangerous because it can weaken the bond of the wheel as it is worn thinner in one section. Some of the new gouge configurations are difficult to grind. However, the maker of the Glaser Tools offers a jig and system that make repeatable hollow-grinding on the face of the wheel relatively easy.

Fig. 3-17   A chatter tool.

Fig. 3-18   Chatter tool in use.

Fig. 3-19   The multiple-tip shear scraper by Sorby Tools has interchangeable flat H.S.S. tips and double-ended cobalt steel tips that attach to a tool holder of a half-round cross section. This one tool permits aggressive hollowing with a small swivel tip of 45-degree shear scraping with round or square cutters.

Fig. 3-20   A close-up of the round and square H.S.S. tips.

Fig. 3-21 End grain hollowing with a Sorby multiple tip scraper. Here, the tool is being used with an adjustable small tip and the flat surface of the tool holder shank sits firmly on the tool rest.

Fig. 3-23 Using a curved-edge tip for shear scraping the inside of a bowl. *Photo courtesy Robert Sorby Tools.*

Fig. 3-22 Scraping with a Sorby multiple-tip tool. Here, the rounded shank of the tool is held on the tool rest to present the straight cutter at about 45 degrees to the outside of the work for a light shear scraping cut.

Fig. 3-24 Scraping in the hollowing of an end-grain turning. Note the fine shavings. *Photo courtesy Robert Sorby Tools.*

Fig. 3-25 Another tool system with interchangeable cutter and handle components by Robert Sorby Tools is marketed as the "R2000 System."

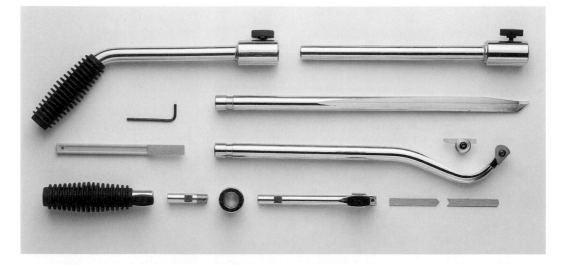

Fig. 3-26 This Sorby "Slicer" (part of the R2000 System) features a tungsten carbide tip that permits deep plunge parting type cuts to remove cone-shaped cores from bowls, thus conserving and making smaller bowls from the otherwise waste. *Photo courtesy of Robert Sorby Tools.*

Fig. 3-27 Bowls all made from one blank separated by the Sorby slicing tool.

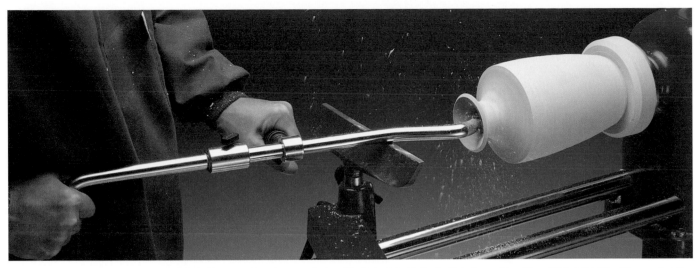

Fig. 3-28   A hook-shaped tool designed for hollow vessel turning manufactured by Robert Sorby Tools. Note the multiposition side handle placed to counteract rotational force. This hollow vessel tool (with adjustable H.S.S. cutter) as others of this general design must be used with the tool rest supporting only the straight portion of the tool, not any part of the hooked or curved end. Thus, the tool rest is some distance from the workpiece. *Photo courtesy of Robert Sorby Tools.*

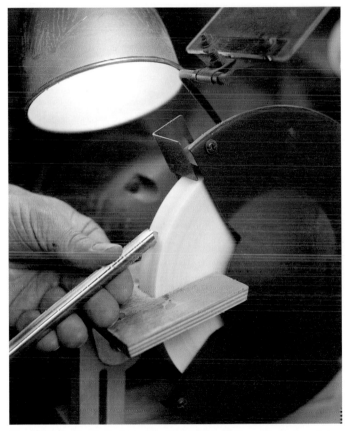

Fig. 3-30   Grinding a roughing gouge on an 80-grit, self-adhesive aluminum oxide abrasive sheet lathe mounted on a plywood or MDF disc. This technique enables the user to see the bevel at all times throughout the rolling manipulation of the tool. *Photo courtesy of Robert Sorby Tools.*

Fig. 3-29   Freehand grinding a blunt bevel (45 to 60 degrees) on a deep flute bowl gouge. Notice the light and white 60- or 80- grit aluminum oxide abrasive being used.

The Glaser Grinding Jig (Figs. 3-31 and 3-32) looks fairly complicated to use, but it is accompanied by a clearly written instruction manual. The machine grinds all bevels hollow rather than flat facilitating quick honing by contacting the heel and the edge with a hone (Figs. 3-33 and 3-34). Frequent and subsequent honing assures the sharpest possible edge.

Some turners use their tools direct from the grinder without honing gouges or stroping skews. It is still my belief, though, that to get the sharpest edges, the tools must be honed. Using tools direct off the grinder without honing is okay in early roughing stages of a turning. But to fair out the line, refine the form, and minimize sanding, sharp edges are a must—even more so when attempting to turn dry softwoods. Take a tip from woodcarvers who hone and strop frequently for the sharpest, cleanest cutting and easiest-to-control tool manipulation. Look at a bevel and edge ground on an 80- or 100-grit grinder under a magnifying glass, and you may be surprised at how ragged the cutting edge is (Figs. 3-35 to 3-37).

Fig. 3-31 The Glaser grinding jig allows consistent and repeatable hollow grinding of gouges and other tools on the face of the wheel with a minimum of practice. *Photo courtesy of Craft Supplies USA.*

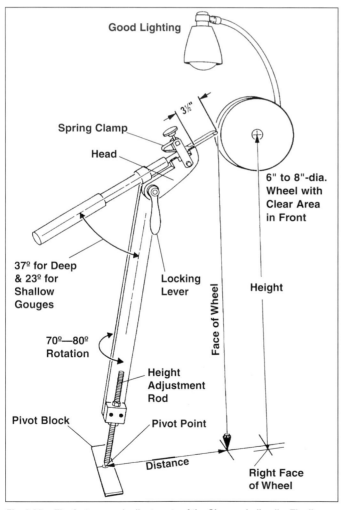

Fig. 3-32 The features and adjustments of the Glaser grinding jig. The jig comes with an easy-to-follow instruction manual.

Fig. 3-33 A close look at a honed gouge shows bright polished metal at the heel and along the edge of this hollow ground tool, which gives it maximum sharpness.

Fig. 3-34 Work the bevel briefly, but all along the edge with an up and down stroke using a diamond or other type hone.

22

Fig. 3-35 Work the inside of the flute with a round hone. The object is to remove the burr without creating a micro bevel inside the flute. This also removes mill marks that otherwise would not present a smooth surface to the cutting edge.

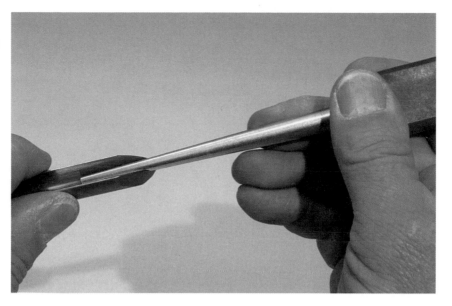

Fig. 3-36 For the ultimate cut, a skew should be very sharp. To achieve and maintain sharpness, use a leather strop and frequently strop between grinding and honing, just as a wood carver or barber frequently strops the knife or razor's edge.

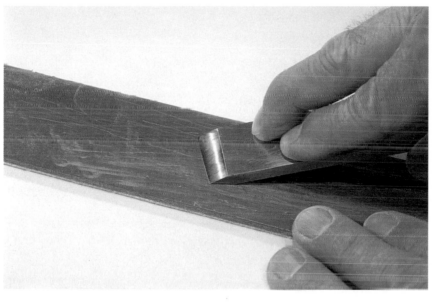

Fig. 3-37 Using an inexpensive 5- to 10-power magnifying glass to inspect tool edges and surfaces they cut. It is an interesting and revealing practice that is highly recommended.

23

Chapter 4

Stock-Holding Techniques

It is well known that the two basic ways of holding wood as it is rotated in the lathe are securing it between the two spindles' centers or screwing it onto a faceplate. This chapter will briefly examine some other methods, which may be new and beneficial to you.

Special Drive Center

(Fig. 4-1) When turning any amount of heavy, wet, green wood between centers, you may find that a typical spur center, because of its small size, will not hold its grip and drive the wood properly because of the soft weak fibers of the wet wood. Often, the starting thrust of the lathe against the heavy load or the leverage of a heavy cut causes a regular spur center to tear away the wood, leaving poor and sometimes dangerous connections to the wood.

A local machine shop can make a modified drive center similar to the one shown in the photo if you provide a sacrificial spur or dead center that fits your headstock spindle. The custom drive center shown here is made with a ¼" x 1½" x 4" flat bar and part of a pointed drill rod welded in place.

Screw Chucks

(Fig. 4-2) Screw chucks are not actually a new idea, but professional turners use them regularly. Since most agree that the Glaser chuck is the best, I want to introduce it to those who may not be familiar with it. Pieces up to 16" in diameter and 4" or so in thickness can be mounted quickly and held securely with this excellent device. Its key feature is its ⅜" stainless steel screw with super-sharp threads. This offers fast and powerful holding. It also features a removable and reversible threaded outer collar (Fig. 4-3) that provides a choice of three different bearing surface diameters: 1½", 2½" and 3½".

Fig. 4-1   A specially made drive center for spindle turning large, heavy wet wood.

Fig. 4-2   The popular Glaser screw chuck features a ⅜" stainless steel screw with very sharp threads.

A very serviceable self-made screw chuck is shown in Figs. 4-4 and 4-5 on page 26. I prefer this for most light- to medium-duty work because I usually do not need to drill a pilot hole for the screw. However, it really requires a dedicated faceplate if used mainly for production work.

Double-Faced Tape

Double-faced tape (Fig. 4-6 on page 26) with a cloth backing has great holding power, and, surprisingly, many turners use it to mount round and balanced turning blanks to faceplates without screws. This is an ideal approach for holding lighter and thin work-pieces, such as plates and platters. There are recommended precautions to observe when using this wood-holding technique:

1. Assure that the wood is dry and both it and the faceplate are clean, flat and free of dust or wax.

2. Brief clamping pressure one to four minutes after applying the tape assures the best possible bond.

3. Before turning on the lathe power, give the blank a pull or two to be certain the bond is adequate.

4. Separation of the faceplate from the finished workpiece is best accomplished with a good putty knife or chisel to wedge the turning free.

5. Use a good grade of double-face tape as some inexpensive types can separate.

6. Don't leave a double-face-taped piece of wood in a vertical position for a long period of time as it will come untaped.

Vacuum Chucking

(Fig. 4-7 and 4-8 on page 26) Many woodworking shops successfully employ vacuum-clamping pressure with great success to press and glue veneers onto flat panels, to form laminated shapes, and to hold templates and jigs firmly in place during machining. Vacuum clamping can be done in faceplate work as well (Fig. 4-9 on page 26). Air pressure at sea level gives a force of about 15 pounds per square inch in all directions. By removing (extracting) air from one side of a flat

Fig. 4-3   Removable and reversible collar of the Glaser chuck provides the turner with a choice of different sizes of bearing surfaces.

Fig. 4-4   A faceplate-mounted screw chuck. Round shims are used to shorten the exposed screw length when necessary.

surface, a natural force of up to 15 PSI will be applied to the opposite side. An electric vacuum pump or a Venturi-type pump (Fig. 4-10 on page 26) that works off of compressed air are the two methods used to evacuate the air. To work, air is drawn out of a shallow chamber formed with special tape to create a vacuum on a faceplate-mounted chuck. The advantage of vacuum-clamping in lathe work is that it is instantaneously fast—on or off just with the turn of a valve. It's ideal for holding thin material. Screw holes, glue, tape, or other time-consuming steps or mess can be totally eliminated for many faceplate jobs.
Electric vacuum pumps are expensive and can be purchased from industrial equipment supply companies.

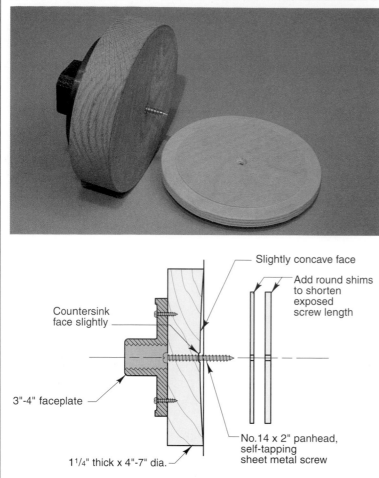

Slightly concave face

Add round shims to shorten exposed screw length

Countersink face slightly

3"-4" faceplate

No.14 x 2" panhead, self-tapping sheet metal screw

1¼" thick x 4"-7" dia.

Fig. 4-5   Suggested details for making your own screw chuck.

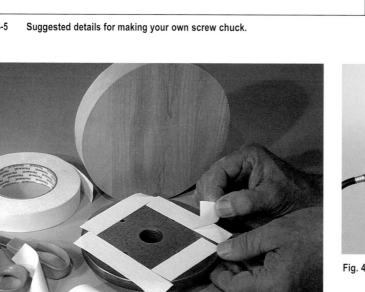

Fig. 4-6   Applying double-faced cloth-backed tape to a faceplate. (Caution! Not all double-faced tapes are the same in thickness and holding power.)

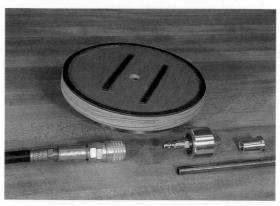

Fig. 4-7   Vacuum chuck components. Above is a lathe vacuum chuck mounted to a faceplate. The vacuum chamber is formed with a special closed-cell foam tape. Note its center air evacuation hole. Below are the air hose, bearing assembly with disconnect, the threaded nose piece, and the continuous ⅛" threaded pipe which fits though the hollow headstock spindle.

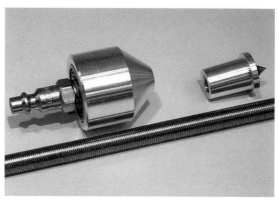

Fig. 4-8   Close-up of the lathe chuck components available from the Turning Post Studio of Ogden, Utah.

Fig. 4-9   The vacuum chucking set-up on my old Oliver lathe.

Venturi-type pumps can be purchased from woodworker's general supply companies and through most major mail order companies specializing in tooling for woodworkers.

Super Glues

Super glues (cyanoacrylate), or "instant" adhesives, are extremely popular among serious woodturners. In fact, it has so many different problem-solving uses for the turner one can hardly survive without it. One of the most popular brands is "Hot Stuff" (Fig. 4-11). It is available from most woodworking supply stores and model shops and by mail order.

The most amazing features of the Hot Stuff adhesive are its ability to glue wet as well as dry wood and its ability to hold end grain. Therefore, it is widely used to attach wet wood blanks to a waste block that's mounted to a faceplate (Figs. 4-12 and 4-13 to 4-18 on page 28).

Hot Stuff is also used to glue unlike materials to wood, to fill cracks, to fortify screw holes in soft or punky wood, and to strengthen weak end grain fibers so that they can be cut or sheared rather than tear away under the tool. Available in different viscosities, this product is certainly a boost when turning any splintery, weak, partially decayed, spalted or any other type of difficult-to-work wood.

Use thick or gap-filling consistency for quickly bonding bowl blanks to waste blocks. A shot of accelerator mist will cure thick beads or fillets of adhesive almost instantly. Use one or several drops to glue unusual material to a waste block for turning. Bone, plastic, and soft metals can thus be turned for inlays and decorative elements to complement your turnings. This adhesive has remarkable shear strength, but, because of its brittleness, the joint can be broken with a quick wedging impact, such as a chisel blow.

Making and Using a Spigot Chuck

(Fig. 4-19 on page 29) A spigot chuck is especially useful for turning end grain of cylinders when making vases, lidded boxes, and goblets. I made my spigot chuck to be used with the Glaser screw chuck because I didn't want to dedicate a faceplate to it or take the time of mounting it to one whenever I needed to use it.

The task is straightforward once a prepared blank is made. I made mine from a glue-laminated chunk of ¾"

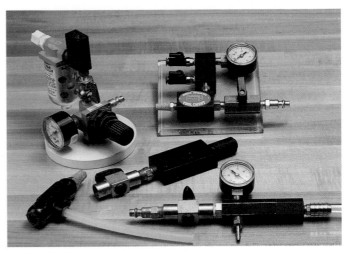

Fig. 4-10 A variety of Venturi-type vacuum pumps that convert compressed air into a vacuum air source.

Fig. 4-11 Super glues (cyanoacrylate), or "instant" adhesives, are available in three different viscosities. The thinner and quicker penetration shown from left to right is evident by observing the placement of several drops on the raw wood in front of each respective container. At the far right is the accelerator which speeds up the glue's reaction time.

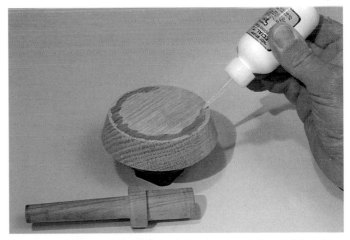

Fig. 4-12 Applying a generous bead of gap-filling Hot Stuff around the edge of a faceplate-mounted waste block. Also shown is a turned positioning jig that fits into the tailstock spindle.

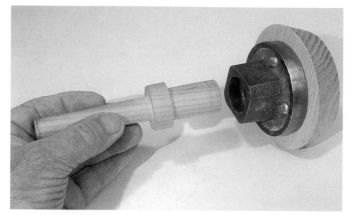

Fig. 4-13   The positioning jig has a stub end sized to fit tightly into the threaded portion of the faceplate.

Fig. 4-14   Here, a typical wet-wood bowl blank is mounted on a faceplate, and, with its outside shape finished, it is ready for precisely centered reverse mounting. The base of the bowl is turned slightly concave. Gap-filling Hot Stuff adhesive is applied to the waste block, and the bowl base gets a shot of accelerator before they are brought together by advancing the tailstock spindle.

Fig. 4-15   After one or two minutes, retract the tailstock, removing the turned positioning plug as shown. Apply several optional fillets around the waste block for an added measure of holding power. Wait 15-20 minutes after applying the accelerator before starting up a heavy turning.

Fig. 4-16   Prepare to turn the inside as usual. Here, a Jacobs chuck holds a bit in the tailstock as a large hole is bored to establish the final depth. In this case, the inside can now be worked extremely close to the bottom because no screws are holding the bowl blank.

Fig. 4-17   Once the bowl is finished, the waste block is carefully removed by wedge-snapping the glue joint with a chisel as shown. Note the downward pressure of the forearm on the faceplate to steady the bowl and that the bowl is placed on a soft rubber pad.

Fig. 4-18   Finally, sand away the glue residue. A slightly concave bottom surface should result; or other work can be done to it at the turner's option.

28

dry white oak boards for dimensional stability. Any good dry hardwood will work. The saw-trimmed starting blank was 4½" square x 4" in total length. I set in a ½"-diameter dowel running across the grain of the blank to provide a good anchor for the threads of my screw chuck (Figs. 4-20 through 4-22). Fig. 4-23 on page 30 shows the spigot chuck and a homemade steady rest in use during an end-grain boring operation in preparation for end-grain shaping.

Homemade Steady Rest

The version shown in Figs. 4-23 and 4-24 on page 30 is fairly easy to make, but cannot be expected to perform like a heavy, cast-iron manufactured one. However, if required only for occasional use and considering the nominal cost for materials, I suggest making one. The steady rest shown in Figs. 4-23 and 4-24 was made to fit a 14" lathe. It can also be made to work on a 12" lathe, as detailed in Fig. 4-27 on page 31. One important construction tip: Rout the 1¼"-wide x ⅛"-deep recesses before sawing the inside and outside circular profiles (Figs. 4-28 and 4-29 on page 31). Figs. 4-23 through 4-26 show a typical vase turning, including end-grain hollowing and shapings.

Four-Jaw Chucks

Four-jaw chucks (Figs. 4-30 through 4-32 on page 32), developed to mount to most headstock spindles of wood lathes, are available from several different sources. Each brand has certain features and optional jaw sets of various sizes and configurations. Essentially, they grip the workpiece by contraction inward or expanding outward. In the latter instance, the jaws apply pressure outward from within a preturned recess cut on a workpiece, such as the bottom of a bowl blank (Fig. 4-30 on page 32). Some have dovetail-shaped jaws which ensure added holding power. When inward pressure is applied, the four jaws squeeze against a preturned tenon similar to the holding action of a spigot chuck. In either case, the tenon (spigot), or recess must be prepared within a certain dimensional range so that the workpiece fits within the travel range of the jaws.

Indexing Jigs and Lathe Router Work

Some lathes have indexing devices built into the headstock. Simply engaging a pin, for example, into a series of holes around a pulley allows the operator to fix the workpiece in a choice of stationary positions. This permits other work to be performed on the turning, such as fluting, beading and so on with the

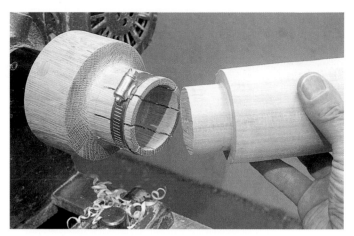

Fig. 4-19 A homemade spigot chuck and a prepared turning project blank with a turned stub tenon that fits snugly and is clamped into the chuck.

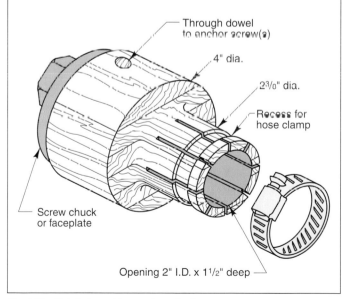

Through dowel to anchor screw(s)

4" dia.

2⅜" dia.

Recess for hose clamp

Screw chuck or faceplate

Opening 2" I.D. x 1½" deep

Fig. 4-20 Details for making a spigot chuck.

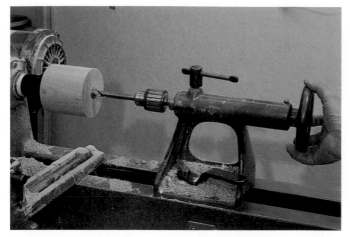

Fig. 4-21　Boring a hole with a machine spur bit to establish the inside depth (1½") of the spigot chuck.

Fig. 4-24　The homemade steady rest supports the work, permitting this end-grain shaping.

Fig. 4-22　The chuck's eight spring fingers (approximately ³⁄₁₆" in thickness) are made with cuts of a handsaw to the full depth of the inside opening.

Fig. 4-25　After finishing the inside of the end-grain turning, the steady rest is removed. The tailstock center provides support with a pad of paper toweling for protection as the rest of the turning is completed.

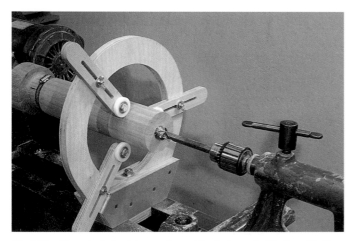

Fig. 4-23　The spigot chuck in use along with a homemade steady rest in the process of making a vase spindle with a hollow end-grain turned top (end).

Fig. 4-26　The vase spindle turned. Here a lamp speeds the drying of a dyed portion as the work spins.

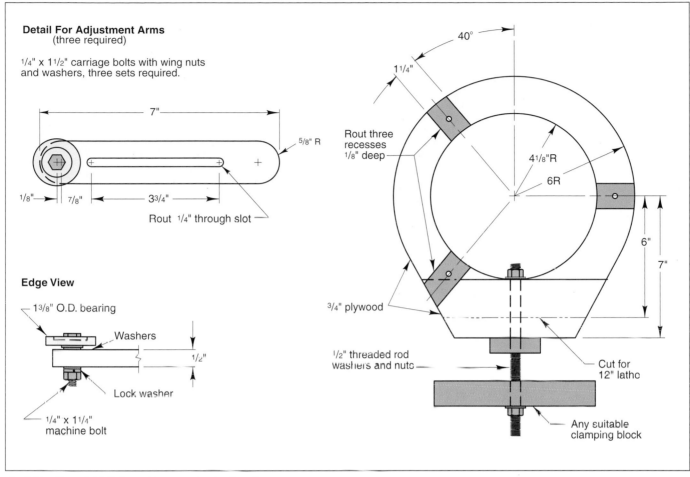

Detail For Adjustment Arms
(three required)

1/4" x 1 1/2" carriage bolts with wing nuts and washers, three sets required.

7"

5/8" R

1/8"   7/8"   3 3/4"

Rout 1/4" through slot

Edge View

1 3/8" O.D. bearing

Washers

1/2"

Lock washer

1/4" x 1 1/4" machine bolt

40°

1 1/4"

Rout three recesses 1/8" deep

4 1/8"R

6R

6"

7"

3/4" plywood

1/2" threaded rod washers and nuts

Cut for 12" lathe

Any suitable clamping block

Fig. 4-27   General details for making your own steady rest.

Fig. 4-28   Make the three adjustable arms first. Tack two strips of wood in position, as shown on each side of an arm piece, to guide the router bit.

Fig. 4-29   A close-up look at the routing guide strips and the bit used. Note that this is a small pattern type of bit with a ½" cutting diameter, 5/16" cutting edge length and a ½" O.D. shank-mounted bearing which rides against the guide strips.

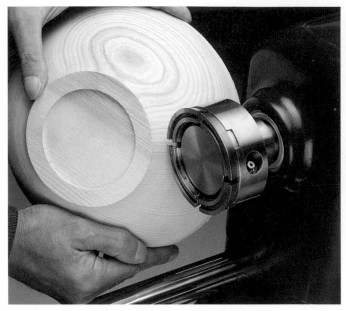

Fig. 4-30　This four-jaw Vantage brand chuck will grip the bottom of the bowl blank. The jaws will expand outward, applying pressure from within the preturned recess. *Photo courtesy of Robert Sorby Tools.*

Fig. 4-32　A close-up of the popular Nova brand chuck. The jaws have a travel of 1" and grips in either the contracting or expanding mode. Accessory jaws are available in a number of different sizes. *Photo courtesy of Craft Supplies, USA, Provo, Utah.*

Fig. 4-31　Turning end grain with the work held in a four-jaw chuck. *Photo courtesy of Robert Sorby Tools.*

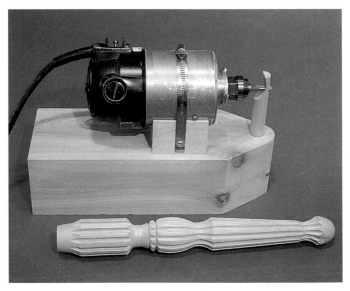

Fig. 4-33　A router sled with a dowel guide nose that permits routing to uniform depth, while following along the in-and-out contours of a turning. Bits of any suitable diameter projects through the dowel guide. The dowel can be interchanged with dowels of any size turned upper diameter or any size horizontal router bit hole as desired.

router or other tools (Fig. 4-33). Indexing and such work should not necessarily be limited to just spindle work. Imaginative surface decoration can also be applied to bowls, platters, vessels and other faceplate work.

If your lathe doesn't have an indexing system, Figs. 4-34 and 4-35 will give you some ideas of how to jig up your own mechanism.

Fig. 4-38 on page 34 shows a lathe routing jig similar to many you may have seen in other books. Jigs of this type are designed for routing on straight cylindrical work of uniform diameter throughout.

A few design differences of the jig shown compared to others are the squared plastic base attached to the router which rides along rabbeted edges, and the manner in which it is designed to extend outside and past the tailstock so that work of many different lengths can be routed with this one jig.

Fig. 4-34   A thin, round indexing plate can be attached to a faceplate for work between centers, providing the spur center protrudes a sufficient distance from the end of the spindle and the surface of the faceplate.

Fig. 4 35   Shown are the necessary easy-to-make components: the thin plywood indexing disc with appropriate line-marked divisions (the lines should extend from the center outward to and over the edge), a horizontal arm clamped to the bed of the lathe and a pivoting connector strip with a reference mark. (When this is clamped to the disc as shown and with the mark on a division line, the work is held at the appropriate position.)

Fig. 4-36   A close-up of a router fluting operation. The sled slides horizontally on a flat surface clamped to the bed of the lathe. The sled moves in and out following the contour of the turning, producing a uniform depth of cut which is controlled by the dowel.

Fig. 4-37   Here is a similar self-made indexing fixture that works on the outboard side. This setup permits work to be done on faceplate-mounted stock. The trick is to devise an anchor for the pivot arm. Here, the jig is clamped to the headstock housing. It could also be fastened to the bench, wall or floor.

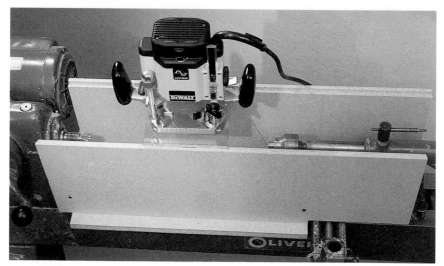

Fig. 4-38   A typical jig for routing and fluting of straight cylinders. Note how the two vertical router support panels extend outside and beyond the tailstock. This permits work of different lengths to be routed with this single jig.

Chapter 5

Wood Materials for Turning

Most woodturners quickly learn that turning softwoods is more difficult than hardwoods. Softwood fibers tend to tear or crush unless cut and severed cleanly with a properly sharpened and properly manipulated tool. Expert turners also find that it is easier, faster and cleaner overall to turn green or wet wood than it is to turn dry wood. This is why, in their videos and books, beautiful and very impressive, endlessly long shavings from wet wood are shown streaming effortlessly from their turning tools. Furthermore, the cost, if any, of green or found wood is minimal and it is usually easily available locally.

To the novice, problems associated with wet wood, such as drying, shrinkage, distortion, and cracking, appear to be insurmountable. Still, to become a successful turner, dedication to learning techniques and peculiarities associated with turning wet wood is a must.

Although the majority of turners prefer to turn green wood, the fact is, that with sharp tools and good technique, almost any material, in any condition that can somehow be held and safely rotated in the lathe can be made into a piece that is practical, aesthetic or both. (See Dewey Garrett's discussion on turning palm wood on page 117.) Apart from green wood are a variety of wood-related and other materials, including plywoods, particle board, MDF (medium density fiberboard), various plastics, bone, nuts, cork, leather, shells and soft metals. However, solid wood remains, by and large, the choice of most artistic turners and buyers of turned art objects.

In the following paragraphs, I'll take a quick look at some materials you can purchase for turning. I'll also suggest a few ideas on how to harvest, store, treat and work with nearly-free local green or wet wood in preparation for turning. I will then examine a new, but not yet publically revealed, nonchemical wood-seasoning method. I hope that this remarkable method

will soon be made available to the general public so that all wood users can harvest, store, and utilize wood in log or board form without degrade.

Project Kits

There are many commercially produced kits, including all of the necessary hardware and wood blanks, some with plans and instructions, available by mail-order purchase for the amateur and hobbyist turner (Fig. 5-1). There are also a wide variety of kits for wooden and plastic craft items, including twist pens and pencils, fountain pens, pepper mills, kaleidoscopes, clocks, music boxes and numerous other items.

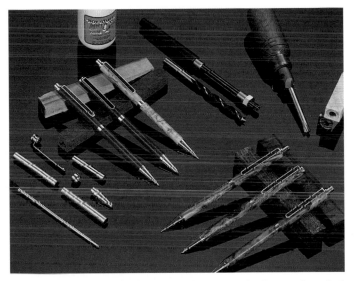

Fig. 5-1   Wood pen and pencil blanks with necessary hardware make up just one type of many woodturning craft kits available from mail-order sources. *Photo courtesy Craft Supplies USA.*

Bowl Kits

Bowl kits, consisting of precut pieces of exotic woods and veneers ready to be glued and turned into elegant, but small segmented bowls, are available by mail order. The kits are designed by Bud Latven for

The Bowl Kit Company. Each kit comes complete with instructions and all the necessary pieces. Currently two kits are available (Figs. 5-2 to 5-5) from a variety of mail sources, including Woodworker's Supply, Albuquerque, New Mexico, and Woodcraft Supply, Parkersburg, West Virginia. For those who are able to obtain and prepare their own component pieces, Bud Latven and The Bowl Kit Company also offer instructional packets for making three different "constructed" bowls, shown in Fig. 5-6 through 5-8. The packet comes with a full-size template/pattern and clear directions that list the materials needed (suggested woods) and provide instructions for making stave components and gluing up the pieces.

Fig. 5-4   Bud Latven's Anasazi bowl kit design features purple heart, holly, and other exotic woods.

Fig. 5-2 This pinstripe bloodwood segmented bowl was made from a kit of premachined components.

Fig. 5-5   Anasazi bowl kit.

Fig. 5-3   The pinstripe kit has all the necessary wood parts precut.

Figs. 5-6, 5-7 & 5-8   Instructional packets available from The Bowl Kit Company contain illustrated step-by-step directions with full-size pattern/templates for making these bowls designed by Bud Latven using woods of your choice.

Fig. 5-7   Segmented bowl in Brazilian purple heart.

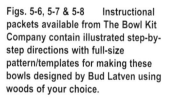

Fig. 5-6   Pinstripe bowl featuring African wenge, holly and ebony.

Fig. 5-8   A herring bowl design featuring a burl (maple) and various exotic hardwoods.

36

Figs. 6-8 and 6-9 on page 45 show an easy-to-make lathe sanding jig accessory, which can be used to prepare and fit the segments that make up many of these types of bowls. Fig. 5-9 shows some built-up spindle turning stock made by gluing various pieces edge to edge or face to face.

Solid Bowl Blanks

Blanks, or chunks of solid wood (Fig. 5-10), prepared for making bowls can be purchased via mail order or prepared at home from your own wood lot or from other local sources. Imported and domestic exotic woods are also available. They are usually totally sealed with a plastic or paraffin coating to prevent degrade from drying due to loss of moisture. These are almost always full of moisture and coated in some manner to keep in the water and prevent the blank from drying and incurring checks and cracks.

Cutting and Preparing Solid Wood Blanks

Stock for small spindle turnings can be cut directly from dried boards, turning squares or rounds. Stock up to 3½" square can be kiln-dried and purchased as dried blanks. Blanks used to make baseball bats are an example. The ends of the chunk of wood can also be coated and allowed to slowly air-dry (Figs. 5-11 to 5-13). For most turnings, it is best not to include the pith or center, of the log, unless, from experience, you know that a branch or particular bolt will not split (assuming you don't want a split). Dead, but standing, trees and cut firewood piles are good sources for turning stock.

Fig. 5-9   Some laminated pieces for spindle turnings.

Fig. 5-10   Solid wood bowl blanks, some purchased and some self-harvested. Notice they are either totally or partially encapsulated with wax or wood sealer to control drying and degrade of checking, splitting or insect infestation.

Fig. 5-11   A solid chunk (or bolt) of birch split off a log section firewood-style and allowed to air-dry before tuning it into a candlestick.

Fig. 5-12   Generally, it is best to avoid blanks that contain the pith, or center, of the log. These will almost always result in a radial split when drying, unless treated in some special manner.

Softwoods usually air-dry faster than hardwoods, and generally the typical drying rate is one year per 1" in thickness. Some 2"-thick hardwood stock may take four times as long, depending upon the species and surrounding humidity. Monitoring the weight is one way to determine when maximum drying is achieved. The weight will change very little over the course of several weeks or months.

A moisture meter (Fig. 5-14) is a good accessory which eliminates the guesswork and gives a precise moisture content evaluation.

Preparing log chunks for bowls and other large turnings involves chainsaw work which should not be undertaken without proper safety instruction (Figs. 5-15 and 5-16). When harvesting bowl blanks from logs where the structural integrity has been altered by insects, worms, spalting or decay, there may be fewer problems with the pith area, as long as the bowl walls are turned relatively thin. Otherwise, for beginners, it is best to prepare bowl blanks working around the pith—excluding it completely from the bowl.

I like to work on a special saw horse when chain-sawing log cut-offs into bowl blanks. A specially prepared board is attached to a regular saw horse. This board has two short lengths of 2 x 4 nailed to one corner. It also has three nails projecting upward, onto which I can slam down flat surfaces of chunks. This holds a chunk safely as I cut off corners or roughly shape the exterior of a bowl blank (Figs. 5-17 to 5-19).

Fig. 5-14 A moisture meter gives an exact reading so that the turner knows what reaction to expect from the finished turning when completed and in use.

Fig. 5-15 Two unusual conditions of wood that make interesting and popular turnings, Left: "Wormy" in butternut, and Right: "Spalting" of maple. Caution: The fungi that gives spalted wood its beautiful structural decaying process may cause various and severe allergic reactions in some people. Proper dust filters and eye and skin protectors should be used.

Fig. 5-13 Blanks prepared for making cork bottle stopper projects were cut from kiln-dried 2 x 2s and sections of air-dried tree branches. Note the dowel which is held in the Jacob's chuck for turning.

Fig. 5-16 Dividing a log cut-off with the chain saw. Note that the board attached to the saw horse has two short 2 x 4s fastened at the corner, and note the three nails protruding upward to the right. These are normally covered with a piece of scrap when not in use. Also note, in the lower right of the photo, the chunks placed in plastic bags for short-term storage.

38

Fig. 5-17   Removing corners of a bowl blank.

Fig. 5-18   Using the chain saw to balance and rough-shape the outside of a bowl blank.

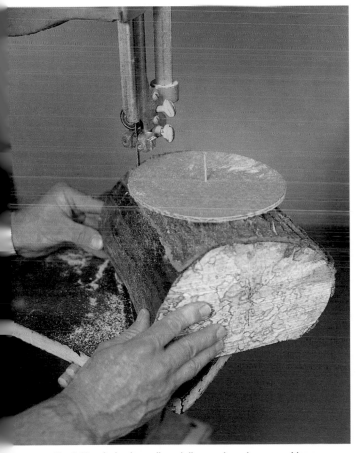

Fig. 5-19   A simple cardboard disc used as shown provides an accurate cutting guide when preparing blanks that are to be uniformly round and well balanced.

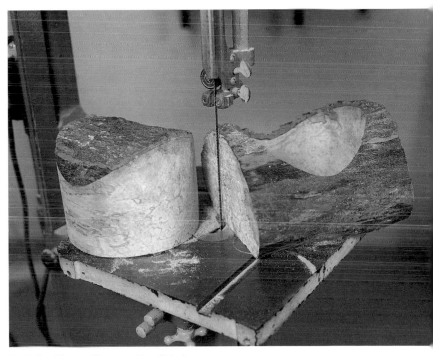

Fig. 5-20   The resulting round bowl blank.

The bandsaw is sometimes helpful but not necessarily required if you have a heavy, solid lathe. Mounting large, out-of-round or irregularly shaped pieces of green or wet wood on lighter-duty lathes is dangerous. In all cases, the workpiece should be prepared as true to round as possible and be quite well balanced in the lathe at start-up (Fig. 5-20 on page 39). Use a slow speed to start.

Once the rough blank has been cut and is ready for the lathe, the wood should be turned immediately or prepared for indefinite storage. All surfaces can be coated with melted paraffin wax, heavy paint, tar or a special wood sealer that is a water-based wax-type emulsion. It's best not to store wood blanks long-term in sealed plastic bags, as this encourages and sprouts mold, mildew and fungus in a short time.

Unfortunately, kiln-dried or dimensionally stabilized wood blanks thicker than 2" are seldom available, if at all. Blanks cut from old, dead trees that were stored and dried slowly for several years are still seldom less than 10 to 12 percent moisture and essentially must be considered green and worked as such. Generally, there are two options: The first is to make a bowl from start to finish from green or wet wood turning thin walls and finishing it in one continuous progression; the second, and probably the easiest for the novice wood turner, is to partially turn the bowl to a rough shape and then carefully dry it before it is finish-turned at a later time. In the latter situation, the bowl is turned so that its walls and bottom are approximately the same thickness in the ¾" to 1" range. Then the roughly shaped blank may be dried or seasoned by various methods. The rough turning will usually distort during drying. The amount and direction of wood movement depends upon the bowl's center axis in relation to the grain orientation of the log and the type of wood.

Seasoning Rough-Turned Bowls
There are numerous techniques woodturners employ to dry or cure rough-turned bowls and vessels. Some methods include the following brief descriptions, but be forewarned that each system must be tested and perfected by the individual turner. The varying density of different wood species and local conditions such as environmental humidity are just a couple of many significant variables.

Some turners, to slowly dry their rough-turned works, bury them in a pile of moist lathe shavings, and one turner actually buries the bowls in manure. Another turner keeps rough-shaped bowls in a plastic bag, which is turned inside out every day or so to remove the moisture vapor that condenses and clings to the inside of the bag. Another also uses a plastic bag with the variation of cutting slits in it so that the moisture can escape slowly.

One of the most interesting bag versions includes inserting a disposable baby diaper along with the rough-turned green bowl. Modern diapers have a "super absorber" that is actually polyacylate, a chemical polymer, which reduces vapor pressure so that moisture condenses on the diaper and is sucked into its fibers.

Another drying technique employed by a turner who made large lamp bases utilized a household dehumidifier in a boxlike chamber to remove moisture. Many individuals have experimented with microwave drying, but documentation assuring its success is scarce. One simple system which has been used successfully is applying the rough-turned bowl all over with a thick coat of paste wax, and then setting it aside for at least six months in a warm—but not too dry— environment.

One of our highly experienced and renowned featured turners puts a clamp around the rough-turned bowl. If the bowl design is such that a clamp might slip from a curved surface, he prepares the rough–turned bowl so that it has a flat area for the clamp. He uses a "plumber's band" (hose clamp) and tightens it slightly every day. After checking the weight of the bowl, he knows the blank is dry and ready for final turning when the clamp will not tighten any further.

Seasoning with Polyethylene Glycol 1000, also known as PEG, may have applications for some turners. Phil Moulthrop uses this substance in his work on page 140. PEG is a hygroscopic waxlike material that is dissolved in water and used to treat rough-turned bowls and other items by an immersion process. When applied properly, the wood will not shrink, crack or distort. It is dimensionally stable. The PEG displaces the moisture in the microscopic latticelike structure of the fiber walls. The treated wood will not take on or lose moisture regardless of local environmental humidity conditions.

There are many disadvantages of using PEG. It is quite expensive and is difficult to finish. Additionally, it does not work well with many conventional finishes.

Some surfaces, if overtreated at all, will become greasy and moist in environments with high relative humidity of 90 percent or above.

PEG works best on fresh green wood, rather than partially dry wood. PEG treatment does not work equally on all woods. Heart wood of hard maple and white oak are nontreatable. In short, the denser the wood, the more difficult it is to take an effective light PEG treatment. Treatment or soaking periods vary from overnight to two months or more, depending upon temperature, concentration of the mixture and the wood's density.

On the plus side of PEG, low-density woods, such as butternut (Fig. 5-21), have been treated successfully with just a 12- to 24-hour treatment at 140 degrees Fahrenheit. The treated wood can be dried in a household oven (Fig. 5-22). Successful PEG treatment holds the bark on. PEG is nontoxic (some pills are covered with it, and it is used in body creams and lotions). Two of the most common problems associated with PEG are that most people tend to overtreat, leaving the wood soaking too long, and that they begin using PEG on hard dense woods before they gain experience with easier-to-treat, lower-density species. For more in-depth information, refer to my book, *Working Green Wood with PEG*, Sterling Publishing Co., Inc., 1984. PEG is available from several of the major woodworking mail-order companies.

ESP-90 Wood Treatment

"ESP-90" is the acronym for the Eugene Sexton Process of 1990. This is a relatively new and unknown wood-treatment process, supposedly perfected in 1990 after years of experimentation and testing of a secret, simple and inexpensive four-step process. Word of its possibilities and importance has been gaining increasing interest among wood users of all kinds nationwide. If this process is actually viable, its potential is far more dramatic and far more encompassing than anything introduced to the wood-using community thus far (Figs. 5-23 and 5-24).

The catch is that the treatment and details of how it functions are not available without paying a substantial sum of money. However, woodworkers who have seen, worked and tested a variety of wood samples treated with ESP-90 are convinced that something very special has happened to the wood. Moisture has been removed from the wood without the use of chemicals and without incurring normal

Fig. 5-21   Green butternut projects that were PEG-treated more than 20 years ago remain dimensionally stable regardless of the grain direction orientation. Note that one bowl and the lamp base were turned on the pith's center axis. The other bowl with two "eyes" was turned from a tree crotch.

Fig. 5-22   More rough-turned, PEG-treated works in butternut just removed after six hours of drying in a household oven at 150 degrees Fahrenheit. Note the holes drilled upward in the lamp base to provide for deeper penetration of PEG.

Fig. 5-23   This 1990 ash container with an end grain lid turned by Eugene Sexton shows no normal drying stress distortion. The bolts of wood also treated in 1990 include walnut, elm, sycamore, white dogwood, white ash and soft maple. These are a few of 68 species which have been successfully treated to date.

41

checking or cracking that develops in wood used or stored in the log form.

In 1991, ES TECH, Inc. of Carrollton, Georgia, was incorporated for the express purpose of marketing and protecting the ESP-90 process. The claims of the process as printed in ES TECH published data are as follows:

A. Control and/or eliminate the blue stain in wood (Fig. 5-25).

B. Eliminate the checking and splitting defects caused by conventional methods of drying wood.

C. Dry various species of wood to 8 percent moisture content without utilizing the conventional drying techniques.

According to ES TECH, Inc.:
"The ESP-90 process and its derivatives do not require any chemicals or specialized equipment to accomplish any of the results mentioned above. Furthermore, ESP-90 is safe, non-toxic, non-polluting and economical. As an example of the economics involved, a tree of any species and girth or height can be processed for less than a dollar per tree at a rate of approximately 100 trees per man day."

Currently ES TECH, Inc. is pursuing the United States Government to purchase the process for public domain. Just imagine how great it would be to be able to stockpile wood in log form until you're ready to use it. Imagine, too, the treat of eliminating such problems as cracking, warping, and decay. Although this all sounds too good to be true, I suggest you contact your government officials and encourage them to pursue appropriate exploratory investigations. If something this good does exist, this country and its negatively impacting wood resources cannot afford to let this be detained any longer. Note: See Sexton's massive turning project on pages 145-146.

Fig. 5-24   Sexton's process, ESP-90, permits storage of wood in the log form without decay, stain, insect infestation, cracking or splitting degrade.

Fig. 5-25   Two slices of slash pine from the same tree. Compare the one at left without any treatment to the one on the right which was treated with ESP-90. Both logs were stored together since October of 1994. Slices were removed from the logs in April of 1995. Also shown is a pine turning from ESP-90-treated wood, indicating that all softwood turnings can be enhanced as well as hardwoods.

Fig. 5-26   A close-up of an unfinished slash pine turning made by the inventor of the ESP-90 process, Eugene Sexton.

Chapter 6

Sanding, Texturing & Finishing

Preparation

Professional and experienced turners do as little sanding as possible. Sanding not only creates troublesome dust, but excessive sanding can actually make a piece uneven and out of round. Because of the wood's grain structure, it will abrade faster on the side or flat grain and the areas around knots than on the edge or end grains and the knots themselves. In the case of many softwoods, such as cedar, pine, redwood and fir (as well as some hardwoods), the softer spring growth will abrade away faster than the denser summer growth.

Employing the sanding process to give final shape to an object is generally not good practice. In such instances, the resulting surfaces will be bumpy. Bowl rims, for example, will result in telltale thick and thin edges. This is a definite sign that the final shape was arrived at with excessive abrasive shaping rather than skillful gouge or chisel work.

Sanding to smooth a surface that has cracks or punky or torn fibers is often a wasted effort. These conditions should be rectified in the very early stages of a turning (Figs. 6-1 and 6-2). If not, repeated tear-out (usually below the surface) is likely because of the weakness of the adjoining, supporting fibers.

Small-Disc Sanding

The recommended method of sanding is using the popular power-sanding technique, which utilizes small-diameter abrasive discs on foam-rubber pads driven by electric hand drills or similar accommodating power tools (Figs. 6-3 and 6-4 on page 44). This method is quick and easy. The double-rotational action of the spinning workpiece and the revolution of the abrasive provides fast, efficient sanding. The best system consists of Velcro and soft foam-backed disc holders that permit quick change to different grits (Figs. 6-5 and 6-6 on page 45). The small diameter of the flexible soft-backed disc holders will conform to most gradual inside curves and

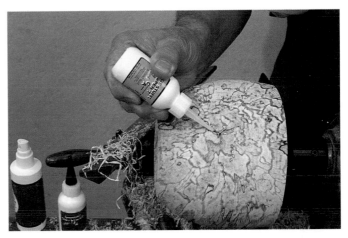

Fig. 6-1   Like some other woods, heavily spalted wood may have voids, a soft pith or cracks which should be repaired early in the course of the turning. Here a gap-filling instant glue is used to fill and toughen the fibers of a pith crack.

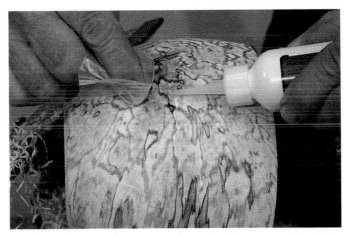

Fig. 6-2   Thinner-consistency super glue penetrates fine cracks. Here, it is spread around to stiffen punky fibers, which otherwise tend to pull and tear away from below the surface. Note the plastic protecting the finger from contacting the glue.

obviously handle outside, convex surfaces. The shop-made sanding balls shown in Fig. 6-4 are useful for sanding inside curves and other dimensionally carved surfaces. Instructions for making them are given in the book, *Making Wood Bowls with a Router and Scroll Saw*, Sterling Publishing Co., Inc., 1992, by myself and Carl Roehl.

Shop-Made Disc Sanders

Sandpaper glued to a thick foam pad that is cemented to a wood disc and mounted on a faceplate or screw chuck is ideal for rounding off the small "nubs" left when parting spindle work from the waste (Fig. 6-7). A scrap of thick carpet padding and some temporary bond spray adhesive is all that's needed.

A flat rigid-face lathe-driven disc sander, such as in Figs. 6-8 and 6-9, has many uses in the shop. I would recommend either a 10"- or 12"-diameter so that you can purchase and use ready-cut discs with preapplied pressure-sensitive adhesive backings. Construct a suitable work support table as shown. Machine an optional ¾"- x ⅜"-deep groove for the table-saw miter gauge. Now you have an effective system for trimming and fitting miter joints as well as for preparing angular pieces for built-up and segmented turnings.

Texturing

Drum sanders (Fig. 6-10) are also useful lathe accessories. A drum-sanding system can be made with a vertical table and used for sanding contour bandsawn cuts of flat boards. It can also be used freehand for texturing convex surfaces, as shown in the photo.

There are many other ways to provide texturing to a turned surface. Repetitive cuts with carving tools that result in a hand-carved appearance is a popular technique. Sometimes just a portion of a turning is textured to give the project a handmade appearance (Fig. 6-11).

Figs. 6-12 and 6-13 on page 46 show a technique for forming small ridges using a short length of a hacksaw blade. The result of light sanding with fine abrasive followed by stain is shown in Fig. 6-14 on page 46. This is also a good technique to use on some tool handles (Fig. 6-15 on page 46).

Making charred lines on spindle work with a wire is an old woodturning trick. This effect is easily accomplished by using a hacksaw frame to hold the

Fig. 6-3   Sanding redwood. This and other softwoods should only be sanded very lightly. Otherwise the work will quickly become out of round because the soft areas abrade away more quickly than the denser summer growth.

Fig. 6-4   Left: A close-up of the 2"- and 3"-diameter Velcro foam-backed sanding discs. Right: These shop-made ball sanders are abrasive-covered soft rubber toy balls developed for sanding inside surfaces by woodworking artist Carl Roehl.

Fig. 6-5 The Velcro sanding system allows quick changing of discs from 60 to 400 grit. *Photo courtesy of Robert Sorby Tools.*

Fig. 6-6   Power sanding the inside of a bowl is easy with the flexible foam-backed disc holders. *Photo courtesy of Robert Sorby Tools.*

Fig. 6-7   This shop-made foam-backed soft sanding disc is perfect for rounding and removing the small nubs that often result when parting off spindle work. Here, it is used to blend and form leather laminated to a tenon of a chisel handle.

Fig. 6-8   A shop-made disc sander consists of an abrasive-faced plywood disc and a simple work-support table. Note the groove cut to receive the table-saw miter gauge.

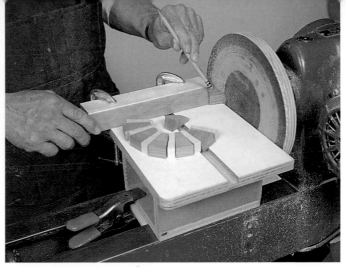

Fig. 6-9   Getting angle cuts of decorative segments ready in the preparation of a layer for a built-up bowl turning.

Fig. 6-10   Texturing as done on the exterior of a turning. A coarse-grit abrasive was used. Then the high areas were hand-sanded with a very fine abrasive so that when stained the texturing was emphasized. The roughened areas absorbed more stain than the smoother, raised ridges.

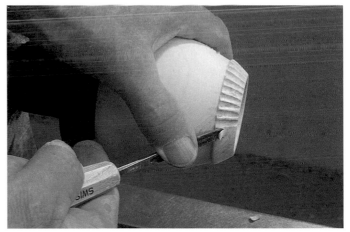

Fig. 6-11   A small gouge is used to decorate around the edge of a small project. The grooves are intentionally nonuniform to give the piece a hand-crafted appearance.

45

Fig. 6-12 A length of a hacksaw blade held in a vice-grip pliers is useful as a texture scraping tool.

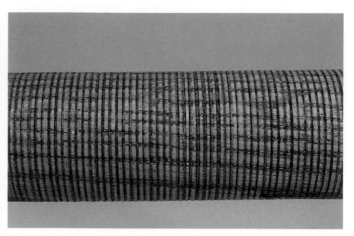

Fig. 6-15 Hacksaw texturing on a tool handle.

Fig. 6-13 Applying the hacksaw blade to the rotating work.

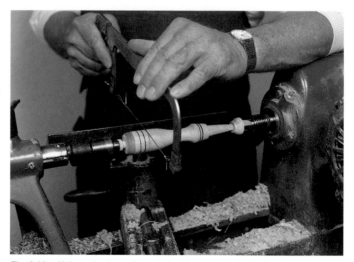

Fig. 6-16 Using a hacksaw frame to hold a taut wire to friction-burn decorative lines around a chisel handle.

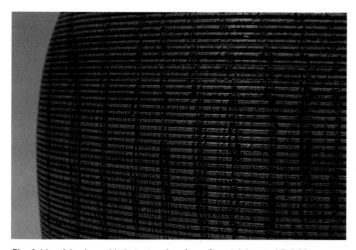

Fig. 6-14 A hacksaw-blade-textured surface after staining and finishing.

Fig. 6-17 Simple to intricate designs can be burned into surfaces. As a rule, closed-grain, light-colored hardwoods work better than softwoods.

wire taut (Fig. 6-16). One option to consider for decorating and texturing the surfaces of some woods is wood burning. Fine, delicate lines, as shown in Fig. 6-17, can be made with a special burning tool.

Entire surfaces or just portions of a turning can be char-textured using a propane torch and steel wool to remove the burned residue. Woods, such as Douglas fir, redwood, southern pine, and cedar, having distinct growth rings lend themselves to this texturing technique (Figs. 6-18 through 6-20).

Sandblast Texturing

Initially, sandblast texturing may seem too involved and not worth the effort, despite the dramatic visual effects that can be achieved with it. However, with just a little straightforward initiative in locating someone who can help or actually do the sandblasting, this can be an exciting and creative process. It's best to either have your own equipment or the services promised from someone else before beginning. Those with sandblasting facilities regularly include autobody repair shops, makers of sandblasted wood signs, tombstone or monument engravers, and general sandblasting contractors and specialists. Checking the telephone directory will provide leads for help and technical assistance.

An illustrated overview is provided of just a few possible applications and essential aspects of the process. A captioned photographic step-by-step procedure for masking and blasting the lamp shown is found on pages 48 and 49 (Figs. 6-21 through 6-38). For much of the staining, finishing and blasting preparation work, it is easiest to keep the project mounted in the lathe.

Some noted turners are having great success by following sandblasting with a wood-bleaching process. This gives the wood a natural weather-beaten appearance—as if it had aged over a long, long period of time. Wood-bleaching kits are available from various sources. The simple texturing and unique design potentials of sandblasting are very appealing for those with creative tendencies. Sandblasting in various woods to various depths and to various degrees of emphasis in combination with stains, colors, bleaches, ebonizing or natural finishes can yield some quite stunning results.

Fig. 6-18 Use a propane torch to char-texture. This is an easy way to add interest and disguise defects of some cheaper softwood species.

Fig. 6-19 The soft areas of the growth rings burn quickly and deeper than the denser areas. Working with the grain lines, use coarse steel wool or a stiff bristle or soft wire brush to remove the residue.

Fig. 6-20 Two samples of char-textured Douglas fir: natural unfinished on the left and stained, clear-finished on the right.

Fig. 6-21   Test samples showing how some hardwoods react to the sandblasting process. Left to right: ash, mahogany, maple, oak, and elm.

Fig. 6-22   Softwood test samples. Note the results created by different face-grain patterns. All samples received nearly identical exposures to the blasting process. Left to right: edge-grain red cedar, flat-grain red cedar, flat-grain slow-growth redwood, edge-grain fast-growth redwood and flat-grain fast-growth redwood.

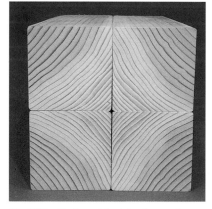

Fig. 6-23   Try to match grain all around when dealing with built-up turnings for sandblasting. Here, four lengths cut from the same redwood 4 x 4 are arranged so that all have the same orientation to the center axis with much of the edge grain exposed.

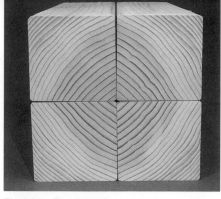

Fig. 6-24   The alternative arrangement would result in a turning having more of a flat-grain blasted pattern.

Fig. 6-25   The lamp base turned, sanded (minimal), stained and finished with several coats of lacquer or urethane finish ready to be prepared for blasting.

Fig. 6-26   The sandblast stencil is like a tape with a protective liner. It comes in rolls of different types and thicknesses and with low-, medium- and high-tack adhesive on vinyl or rubber. Rubber stretches better over compound curves than vinyl. Shown is a medium tack, 30-mil rubber Anchor Continental product No. 120.

Fig. 6-27   Cut the stencil about ⅜" to ½" wider than the flat blasting area to be covered. Note how the rubber edges stretch upward against the turned bead. The liner is removed slowly as the stencil is pressed down.

Fig. 6-28   After the stencil is applied all around and slightly lapped over its starting edge, tape down some carbon paper as shown.

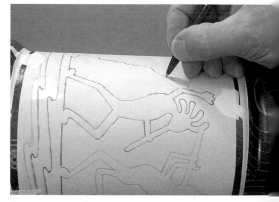

Fig. 6-29   Tape down the pattern, assuring it does not slip in place. Trace the outline of the pattern with a fine ball-point pen.

Fig. 6-30   Remove the pattern and carbon paper. Now carefully cut the stencil using a craft knife as shown. Peel away the stencil from the areas that are to be blasted.

Fig. 6-31   Apply some narrow strips (about ¾" to 1") of stencil, overlapping successive pieces to cover the bead areas. Add more stencil as needed to assure that all areas will be well protected from the powerful blasting stream.

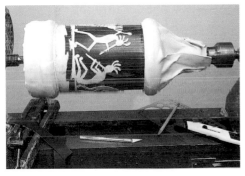

Fig. 6-32   The lamp ready for blasting.

Fig. 6-33A Wait! Before blasting, make some practice runs on flat boards or some other turnings. Here is a white cedar practice turning with its entire surface blasted. Note the knot.

Fig. 6-33B Red cedar practice piece with some design features protected with area masking.

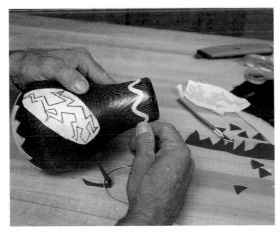

Fig. 6-34   Small areas can be masked with separate pieces of stencil as shown. Note the decorative line application using precut narrow strips of rubber stencil material.

Fig. 6-35   The blasting process. Be sure that all protective body wear is used and other appropriate safety procedures are followed.

Fig. 6-36   Close-up of an area where the blasting is completed.

Fig. 6-37   Removing the sandblast stencil.

49

Fig. 6-38 The completed project. A light application of an appropriate clear spray finish is optional.

Finishing

The first step in finishing is determining the end use of the turning—functional or decorative. In the latter case, almost any type of finishing is permissible, as long as it doesn't fall off the surface or infringe on anyone's right to freedom from visual pollution. Selecting the look you want is indeed a matter of personal taste and artistic expression. Finishes can be very quick and easy or labor intensive, complicated and involved. Some turners use almost instant one-step finishes, and others laboriously build up layers of transparent or solid colors and film-forming hand-rubbed topcoats. Some decorating touches range from incorporating an ebonizing effect (simply coloring a piece black with dyes, stains, ink or paint) to bright gilding with gold leafing. Refer to finishing books and experts for information about complex finishing techniques. Professional production turners prefer the fast, nonlabor-intensive finishes.

Quick and Easy Natural Finishes

Today there are numerous waxes, lathe polishes, and oils available that are basically one-step finishes. Peanut oil (Fig. 6-39), olive oil and other cooking oils are often used with satisfactory results for bowls and turned cutting boards intended for culinary use. Many professionals use waxes or wax and oil combinations. Some one-step waxes are shown in Fig. 6-40 and their easy application is shown in Figs. 6-41 and 6-42. Other popular easy-to-use film-forming finishes are shown in Fig. 6-43.

Painting and Coloring Wood

The lathe is a great aid when adding color to turned wood. Acrylic and other pigmented finishes can be applied to the work as it is held in the lathe and spun under power or rotated with one hand (Fig. 6-44).

Stains and dyes are also used to provide color to sometimes otherwise drab woods. Various colored-water concentrate and aniline dyes (Fig. 6-47) are available that are amazingly easy to prepare and use. Recommended water-based concentrated dye mixtures are 10 percent dye to 90 percent water. These same products can be used to customize colors by adding the dye(s) to water-based finishes. Generally, the procedure for coloring wood with water-based dye is as follows:

1. Raise the grain. Sponge-coat with water, allow to dry and then fine-sand.

2. Re-dampen the surface again just before applying the dye. Wipe out with the grain (Fig. 6-48 on page 52).

3. If necessary, to intensify the color, apply a second coat.

4. Allow to dry. See Fig. 6-49 on page 52.

5. Cut very lightly with steel wool before applying a wax topcoat or other finish (Fig. 6-50 on page 52).

Excellent instruction for producing decorative effects and coloring wood is found in the video *Coloring Wood* by Jan Sanders and sponsored and distributed by Liberon Finishes. This video is available in England from Liberon Waxes, New Romney, in Kent, and in Mendocino, California, from Liberon Supplies.

Novelty Spray Finishes

The convenience and magic of the aerosol spray now offers stone, marble, antique crackle and other unusual finishes almost instantly (Fig. 6-51 through 6-54 on page 52). Flock (not pictured) is another two-step spray finish that is well known. This process involves applying a base of colored adhesive or enamel. While it is still wet, a coating of cotton or rayon fibers dyed the same color is sprayed on the piece. The result is a soft fabriclike finish suitable for coating the bottoms of various turnings. There are also a number of metallic spray finishes available. Ask your finishing supplier or arts and crafts dealer about other new and unusual finishes that might be appropriate for achieving the desired appearance for your turned objects.

Fig. 6-39   Peanut oil is a good finish for bowls intended for culinary use.

Fig. 6-42   When dry, buff with soft cloth. A second application increases surface hardness and shine.

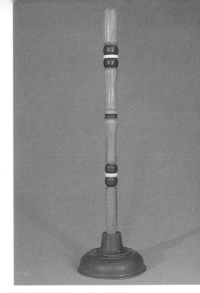

Fig. 6-45   A new handle for an otherwise unattractive home necessity.

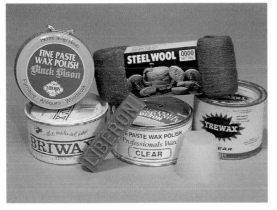

Fig. 6-40   A variety of waxes in paste or stick form. Some are applied with a good quality steel wool—one that is manufactured without grease or oil in long, noncrumbling strands.

Fig. 6-43   Easy-to-use finishes include a penetrating oil among various film-forming types. Note at left the oil confetti light fitted into a simple turned base.

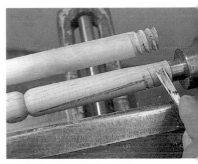

Fig. 6 16   Some utility handles have short threaded ends. These can often be hand-carved to sufficiently duplicate the original which, in this case, is shown above.

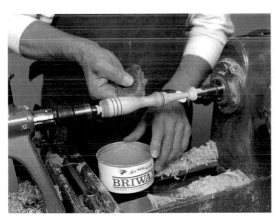

Fig. 6-41   A one-step wax finish. Apply with steel wool or a clean cloth.

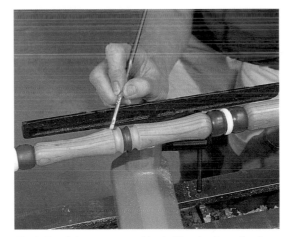

Fig. 6-44   Color accents combined with natural wood make an attractive plunger handle. The acrylic paints are applied with a brush as the work is rotated by hand or lathe power.

Fig. 6-47   Aniline and water concentrate dyes are easy to use and can give spectacular color to otherwise drab wood.

51

Fig. 6-48 Applying water-based dye to a premoistened surface.

Fig. 6-49 A lamp helps to accelerate drying between steps.

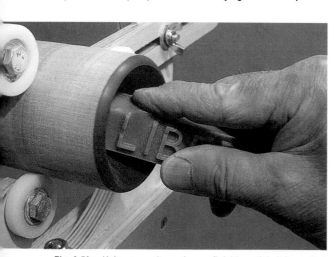

Fig. 6-50 Using a woodturner's wax finishing stick. It is applied as the lathe is turning with moderate pressure and then the surface is buffed with a soft cotton cloth.

Fig. 6-51 Some unusual finishes come direct from handy aerosol cans. Some finishes are applied with common spray finishing equipment. Here a marbleized effect is applied to a vessel.

Fig. 6-52 This marbleized appearance is achieved through an easy two-step process.

Fig. 6-53 This simple candleholder is finished with a two-step stonelike aerosol.

Fig. 6-54 This very interesting two- or three-step crackle finish, available in various colors, creates an instant antique appearance. The size of the cracks is somewhat controllable by the amount of material applied. Left: Lighter coatings result in a greater number of narrow cracks. Right: Fewer but larger cracks result from heavier applications.

Chapter 7

Safety in Turning

The very nature of the woodturning process itself is laden with numerous hazards. You must be constantly aware that injury can result from inattentive use of the lathe and related work. You must also guard against injury from the cutting tools and their sharpening devices, from the possibility of flying waste or splinters of wood, and from the visible waste or shavings as well as from the ultra-fine, invisible airborne particles and fumes that are commonly generated in the turner's environment.

Consider the lathe-held spinning chunks of wood that are often initially heavy and unbalanced. Such work places stresses upon the lathe and the work-mounting system. Into this revolving wood, you then advance a sharp hand-held tool. In the early stages, the tool is not even in continuous contact with the workpiece. It's comparable to shoving something into the spokes of a revolving wheel. Think about it. Most other rotational cutting processes in woodworking are fairly well guarded, or, at least, they should be. Guards as such are available for lathes, but, by and large, they are restrictive and more effective for the protection of nearby observers than they are for the turner.

Mentally, woodturning requires constant concentration concerning the task immediately at hand. Exercise caution and common sense. A turning safely produced on one lathe, for example, may be an absolute catastrophe if attempted on a lighter lathe or if mounted differently. You must know the limits of your lathe, the limits of your material, the limits of your tooling and most importantly, the limits of your own experience.

Be sure to read your owner's manual and follow the manufacturer's recommendations. This, combined with instruction from a qualified professional turning instructor who is familiar with your equipment, are strongly suggested. It is impossible to list every safety "Do & Don't" rule, because there are so many different sizes and capabilities of lathes as well as different possibilities and combinations of circumstances. However, the following are some general safety considerations:

1. Dress properly (Fig. 7-1 on page 54). Tuck in loose clothing and shirt tails, and button down or roll up shirt sleeves. Remove jewelry and tie back long hair.

2. Wear approved eye protection. A full-face shield is better than just goggles. Always wear full eye protection when using super glues.

3. Precheck turning stock, assuring it is free from conditions that might cause it to fly apart or separate from the lathe.

4. Prepare your stock so that it is mounted well—centered and balanced in the lathe. Remove corners from spindles and faceplate work before mounting (Fig. 7-2 on page 54).

5. Always rotate the stock by hand before starting the lathe to make sure that the stock will not jam against the tool rest.

6. Keep the tool rest adjusted as close as possible to the work. Do not make any rest adjustments with the stock revolving.

7. Keep turning tools sharp and well conditioned.

8. Never force a dull tool and avoid heavy cuts. Be sure that all large and irregular shaped turning blanks are started at the slowest speed.

9. Frequently check clamps and the stock-holding system (screws and lathe center tightness).

10. Remove the tool rest when sanding.

11. Do not wrap sandpaper or rags around your fingers. Fold them into pads and apply pressure at one point.

12. Dispose of shavings from mold or spalted woods immediately.

13. Wear an appropriate respirator when working with toxic or chemical finishes.

14. Use water-based finishes whenever possible.

15. Avoid breathing wood dusts.

Microscopic airborne dust particles, invisible to the naked eye, linger in the shop atmosphere for days after turning. Fine dusts from spalted wood, many hardwood exotics, and even a number of common softwoods, such as cedar and redwood and other domestic hardwoods, can be extremely harmful. Certain individuals may react differently initially, but don't chance any respiratory ailment that may not reveal itself for years down the road.

To combat the invisible fine dust particles of bacteria, pollen and fungi, many shop owners are adding auxiliary shop air-filtration systems (Fig. 7-3). These systems are installed in addition to the regular shop vacuum system which extracts sawdust and shavings. This equipment does not remove the fine or microscopic invisible particles that contaminate your shop air. Do not let any potentially harmful dust or fumes enter your lungs.

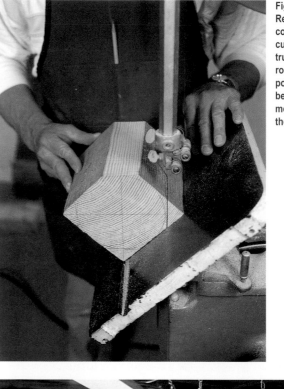

Fig. 7-2 Remove corners or cut stock as true and round as possible before mounting in the lathe.

Fig. 7-1   Some recommended safety practices. Note the snug apron, sleeves rolled up and that eye, face and lung protection is provided by a battery-powered fan incorporated into an impact-resistant face-shield air-filtration unit. Another shop fan in back directs dust toward a vacuum extraction hose positioned near the work. Appropriate lighting assures good visibility.

Fig. 7-3   Ceiling or wall-mounted air-filtration systems such as this are increasingly popular for any woodworking shop. These devices operate quietly and filter the shop air from dangerous invisible dust particles several times per hour, depending upon the shop size, the filter efficiency, fan/motor sizes and CFM ratings.

Chapter 8

Artists' Projects

Patrick Spielman

Patrick Spielman, the author of the previous text, lives surrounded by a natural forest in the famous tourist area of Door County in northeast Wisconsin. A graduate of the University of Wisconsin-Stout, he taught high school and vocational woodworking in Wisconsin public schools for 27 years.

Today, he and his wife, Patricia, own Spielman's Wood Works and Spielman's Kid Works. Both are gift galleries that offer high-quality hand- and machine-crafted wood products produced locally and from around the world.

Patrick left the school classroom 10 years ago, but he continues to teach and share ideas and designs through his published works. He enjoys consulting and lending his knowledge of woodworking to promote the talent and activities of other artisans. He has written over 50 woodworking books with some translated into Dutch and German.

Patrick's love of wood and woodworking began between the ages of eight and 10, when he transformed fruit crates into toys. Encouragement from his parents, two older brothers, and a sister, who provided basic tools to keep the youngster occupied, enabled Patrick to become a very productive woodworker at quite an early age.

One of Patrick's proudest accomplishments is his book *The Router Handbook*, which sold more than 1.5 million copies worldwide. His updated version, *The New Router Handbook*, was selected the best how-to book of 1994 by the National Association of Home and Workshop writers.

Patrick is currently working on a new title, *The Art of the Router*.

Cutting Board

Construction:
1. Glue up and surface blank approximately 1½" to 1¾" thick x 16" diameter.

2. Turn to 15½" O.D. and shape outside edge to suit (see diagram on page 56).

3. Sand edge.

4. Remount the workpiece, shifting the center ½" along grain (length of laminate) with 3-degree wedge between the work and faceplate.

5. Turn and sand, cutting surface and juice groove.

6. Finish with peanut oil.

Cutting Board, black cherry,
15¾" x 1⅝"

Fig. 8-1   This turned cherry cutting board features an off-set turning technique to form the slanted cutting surface and turned juice groove.

Fig. 8-2 Plane a tapered wedge with a 3-degree slant, cut it round and insert it between the workpiece and the faceplate.

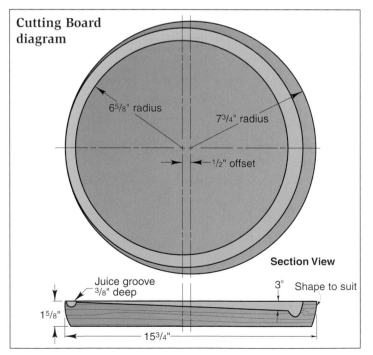

Cutting Board diagram

6⅝" radius

7¾" radius

½" offset

Section View

Juice groove
³/₈" deep

3°   Shape to suit

1⅝"

15¾"

Festive Ornament, unfinished sugar pine, 8¼" H x 2⅛" DIA

Festive Ornament

Construction:

1. Prepare stock 1⅛" x 2¼" x 9".

2. Lay out centers accurately on each end and on faces for the recess (see diagram on page 58).

3. Drill hole through one face at the recess center for mounting on a screw chuck.

4. Mount on screw chuck and turn a recess ¼" deep x 1⅜" diameter on each face. Use a small square nose scraper or a small skew laid on its side to form these recesses. See Figs. 8-4 and 8-5.

5. Mount the workpiece between centers and precisely on centers. Turn to shape, as suggested in the drawing.

6. Use a skew with a shearing cut to form the "round" around the recesses, as shown in Figs. 8-6 and 8-7.

7. Prepare a decorative inset scroll sawn from ¼" stock (preferably cut from the same board). Orient the grain vertically before sawing, and glue in with the grain of the decorative insert running vertically (Fig. 8-8).

8. Leave unfinished or finish as desired.

Fig. 8-3 This unusual project involves turning on a screw chuck and between centers. It also requires a scroll-sawn insert glued into the turned recesses.

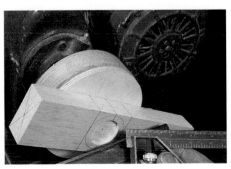

Fig. 8-4 The recess completed on the first face using a homemade screw chuck. (See page 24 for making this screw chuck). Note: An optional shim spacer was used between the workpiece and screw chuck to shorten the protruding length of the screw.

57

Fig. 8-5   Preparing to turn the second recess. Note the shim removed.

Fig. 8-6   Beginning to form around the recess is similar to cutting a large bead with the skew.

Fig. 8-7   A center line drawn across the turned area helps when making the final finishing cuts.

Fig. 8-8   Align the grain of the decorative, sawn cutouts and glue them into the recesses.

Festive Ornament diagram

NOTE: 1 1/8"-thick stock required.

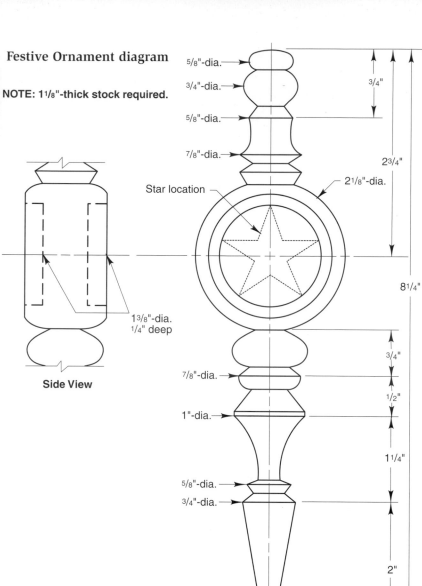

5/8"-dia.
3/4"-dia.
5/8"-dia.
7/8"-dia.

3/4"

2 3/4"

2 1/8"-dia.

Star location

Side View

1 3/8"-dia.
1/4" deep

8 1/4"

7/8"-dia.
3/4"
1/2"
1"-dia.

1 1/4"

5/8"-dia.
3/4"-dia.

2"

Alternate Designs Full Size

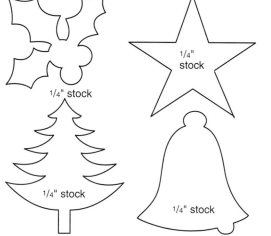

1/4" stock
1/4"
stock
1/4" stock

1/4" stock
1/4" stock
1/4" stock

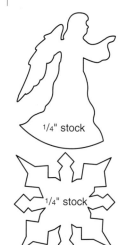

58

Letter Openers,
Lying: walnut, 7½" H
x 1 1/16" DIA;
Standing: cocobolo,
8¼" H x 15/16" DIA

Letter Opener

Construction:
Turn letter openers according to dimensions provided
in diagrams on page 60.

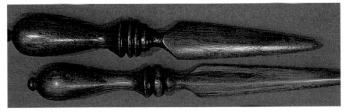

Fig. 8-9   Making these letter opener projects involves basic spindle turning
and hand shaping the blade off the lathe.

Fig. 8-10   After turning the handle and forming the blade round, mark the two
knife edges on the edge grain 180 degrees from each other. Note the tool rest
used as a marking aide.

Fig. 8-11   Using the point of a skew to part it off the lathe.

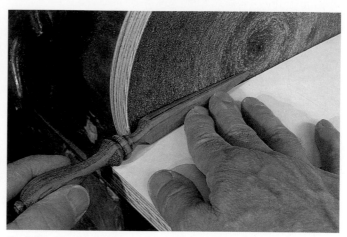

Fig. 8-12   Shaping the blade edges freehand on the homemade lathe disc sander. Sand to the pencil lines. See page 45 for more information about the lathe disc sander accessory.

Walnut Letter Opener diagram

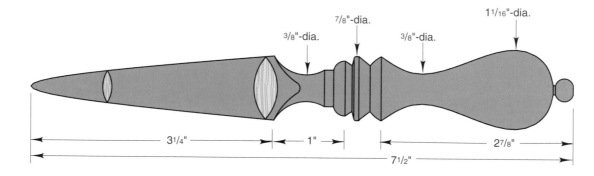

3/8"-dia.

7/8"-dia.

3/8"-dia.

1 1/16"-dia.

3 1/4" — 1" — 2 7/8"

7 1/2"

Cocobolo Letter Opener diagram

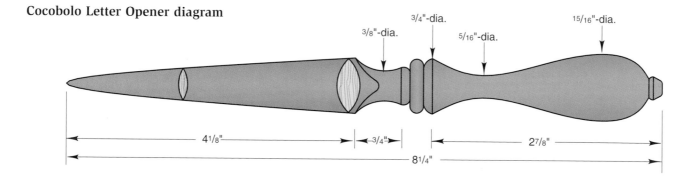

3/8"-dia.

3/4"-dia.

5/16"-dia.

15/16"-dia.

4 1/8" — 3/4" — 2 7/8"

8 1/4"

Ridged Bowl

Ridged Bowl diagram

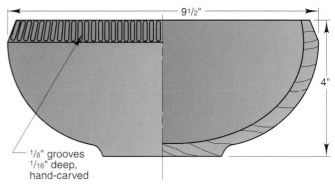

9½"

4"

¹/₈" grooves
¹/₁₆" deep,
hand-carved

Ridged Bowl, mahogany, 4" H x 9½" DIA

Textured Mug

Construction:
Turned rustic mug. All outside surfaces were textured with coarse abrasive on a drum sander. The surfaces were then sanded with fine abrasive, the handle glued on, and stained to highlight the texturing. Turn according to dimensions provided in diagram.

Textured Mug diagram

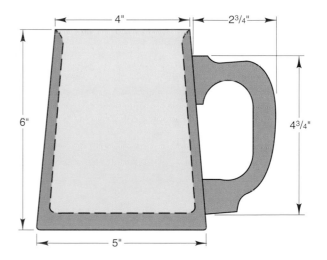

4"   2³/₄"

6"   4³/₄"

5"

Textured Mug, stained white cedar, 6" H x 5" DIA

Potpourri Bowl, ash lid and padauk bowl, 2⅝" H x 5½" DIA

Potpourri Bowl

Construction:
The Potpourri Bowl is made in two pieces. The bottom is a simple bowl. The lid is turned to fit the bowl. Then the pattern is scroll-sawn in the lid. Turn according to dimensions provided in diagram.

Potpourri Bowl diagram

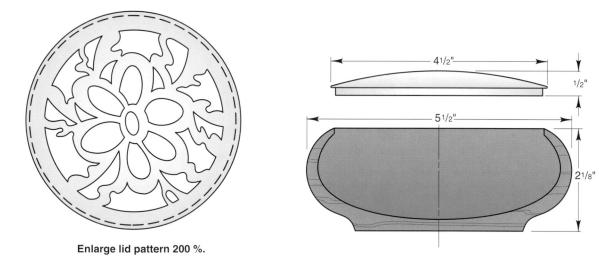

Enlarge lid pattern 200 %.

Wormy Bowl, wormy butternut, 6⅝" H x 8¼" DIA

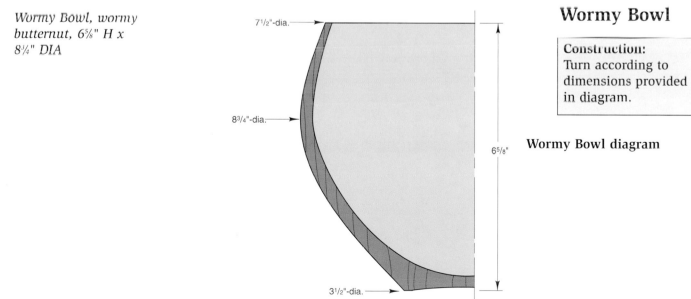

7½"-dia.

8¾"-dia.

6⅝"

3½"-dia.

Wormy Bowl diagram

Wormy Bowl

Construction:
Turn according to dimensions provided in diagram.

Spalted Maple Bowls, spalted maple, Left: 4⅝" H x 6⅝" DIA; Right: 5½" H x 7¾" DIA

Spalted Maple Bowls

Construction:
Turn bowls according to dimensions provided in diagrams.

Left Spalted Maple bowl diagram

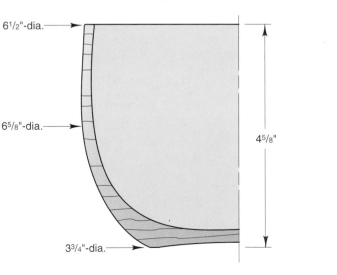

6½"-dia.

6⅝"-dia.

4⅝"

3¾"-dia.

Right Spalted Maple bowl diagram

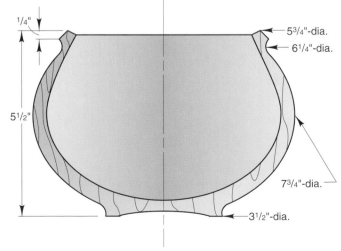

¼"

5¾"-dia.

6¼"-dia.

5½"

7¾"-dia.

3½"-dia.

64

*Butternut Weed Vase,
butternut, 5¾" H x
6½" DIA*

Butternut Weed Vase

Construction:
A weed pot of this shape can be turned from any material. This one is PEG
(Polyethylene Glycol 1,000) treated butternut turned from a tree crotch so that the
grain figure gives the object two pith "eyes." Random holes were drilled upward from
the bottom to facilitate deeper penetration of the PEG.

Southwestern Sandblasted Lamp

Construction:
Turn lamp according to step-by-step instructions shown in Figs. 6-25 through 6-38 on pages 48-50 and dimensions provided in the diagrams.

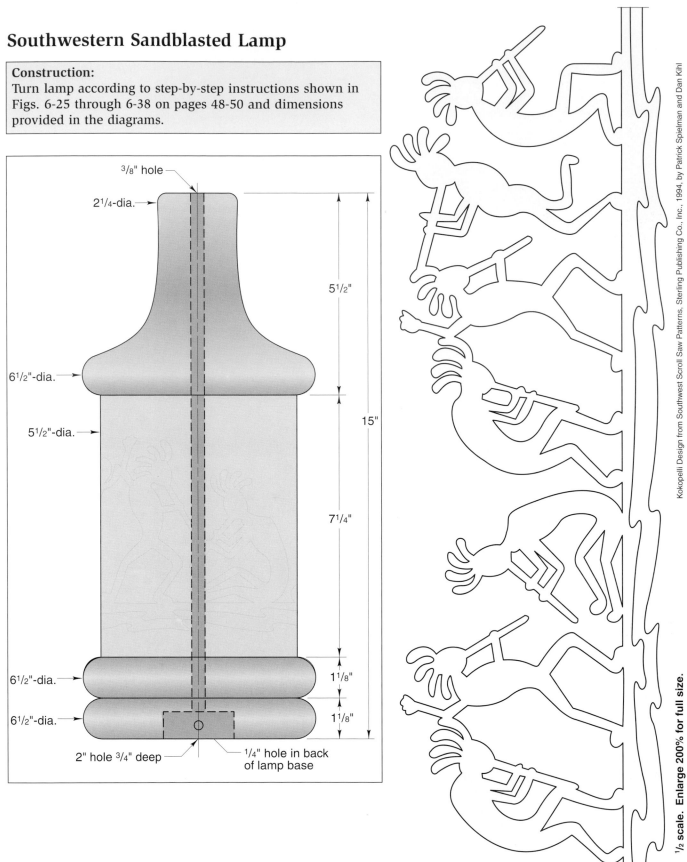

3/8" hole

2¹/₄-dia.

6¹/₂"-dia.

5¹/₂"-dia.

6¹/₂"-dia.

6¹/₂"-dia.

2" hole ³/₄" deep

¹/₄" hole in back of lamp base

5¹/₂"

15"

7¹/₄"

1¹/₈"

1¹/₈"

Kokopelli Design from Southwest Scroll Saw Patterns, Sterling Publishing Co., Inc., 1994, by Patrick Spielman and Dan Kihl

¹/₂ scale. **Enlarge 200% for full size.**

Nick Cook

Nick Cook is a professional woodturner living in Marietta, Georgia, where he owns and operates his studio. He grew up around his father's woodworking equipment. His family claims that he began woodworking when he was tall enough to see over the table saw.

Nick became interested in the art of woodturning in the mid-70s after several years in furniture design and manufacture.

"Turning is the most spontaneous method of making something of wood," says Nick. "The lathe allows much more freedom in shaping wood than any other hand tool."

The primary materials that he now uses are maple, cocobolo and tagua nuts. He employs a variety of woods, both domestic and exotic for his one-of-a-kind pieces. He enjoys turning artistic pieces, but he recognizes that it's the functional work that allows him the luxury of doing so. Popular functional items include wine stoppers, letter openers, baby rattles and French pastry rolling pins. Each item is hand-turned and signed by Nick.

Nick's work is marketed in gift shops and galleries from coast to coast and is included in numerous corporate and private collections.

He is a founding member of the American Association of Woodturners and is the current vice president. He spends much of his time demonstrating and lecturing at universities, craft schools and woodworking shows throughout the country. He also writes articles for several woodworking publications.

Gavel (photo on page 68)

Construction:
Turn gavel according to dimensions provided in the diagram below.

Gavel diagram

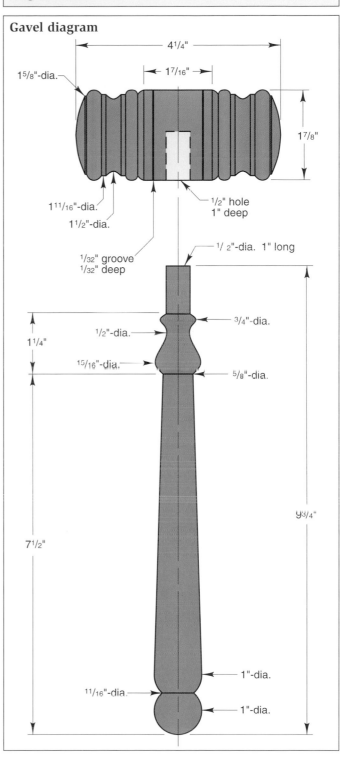

Gavel, cocobolo, 4¼" x 10⅝" H x 1" DIA

Judy Ditmer

photo by Bob Barrett

Judy Ditmer says that she knew she was an artist when she was four years old, but it took a long time to find her medium.

Judy says that as a child she always liked to make things, and to take things apart and figure out how they work. As she followed her interests into an art school, she became a little discouraged. She says she had nearly given up on being able to do art for a living when she discovered woodturning.

"When I first began to make bowls of wood, it seemed to me the most magical thing I'd ever done," she says. She found the process of turning—the complete integration of time and space in the designing and the making of a piece—to be simply wonderful.

Judy began designing and making earrings out of the need to have small inexpensive items to sell at shows and to wholesale to gift shops and galleries. Making these small sculptures has furnished her with endless opportunity to explore form and space, color and line, and iteration and contrast.

Earrings (photo on page 70)

Construction:

1. Using diagrams below, turn a cylinder about 1½" to 2" in diameter with a spigot at one end.

2. Turn a matching recess in a waste block of hardwood mounted on a faceplate. A good fit is essential. Glue cylinder onto the waste block.

3. Turn a concave end grain surface of the disc.

4. Make a clearance cut with a parting tool.

5. Make the final parting-off cut following the curve.

6. Cut the disc into halves or quarters as desired.

7. Finish-sand and shape edges on a drum sander and a small foam-backed disc sander.

8. Drill small holes for bead dangles, posts, ear wires or findings as necessary.

9. Spray finish with clear lacquer.

10. Assemble.

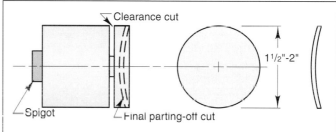

Earrings #1 diagram

2 pieces each

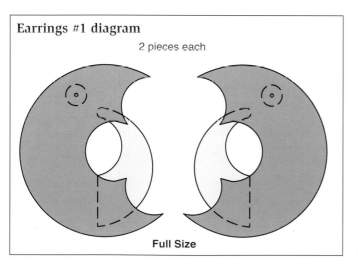

Full Size

Earrings #2 diagram

3 pieces each

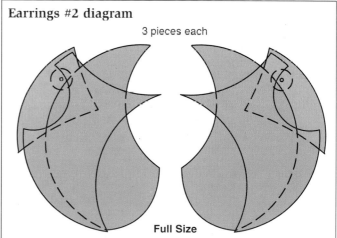

Full Size

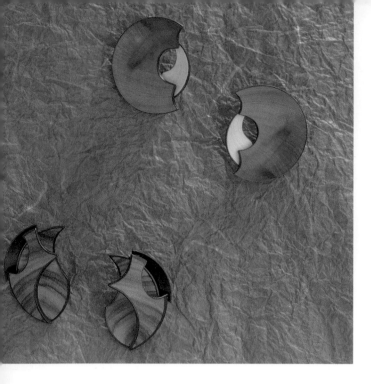

Earrings, African boxwood,
Rose of Sharon, ebony,
tulip wood, largest: 1¾" L

Sculptural Bowl, persimmon, 3" H x
13" W x 15" DIA

Sculptural Bowl,
osage orange,
4¼" H x 13½" W
x 8½" DIA

Thomas Foster

photo by Chris Alexopoulos

Born in 1955, Thomas Foster grew up in the village of Weston, Vermont. His father was a postmaster who kept his own wood shop during afternoon and weekend hours. He made much of the furniture in Thomas's home and sold some other items of wood.

Years later as an English major at an art college, Thomas grew increasingly frustrated with the likes of Shelly and Coleridge and tried his hand at a few ceramic-studio courses. He discovered he had a knack for it, and developed a reputation as the pesky guy who kept the raku pits so busy that the nearby jewelry studio had to keep their windows closed even on a really nice day just to keep the smoke out.

"I found out that clay body, glaze, and shape counted in one art form the same way plot, character, and theme do in another," says Thomas. "I also realized that a few determined people were spending most of their time wrestling with those concerns. They were called potters."

During this time, Thomas worked summers and vacations in his father's wood shop in Weston on various woodworking projects, which he sold at flea markets and local stores. It was here that he accumulated a few tools, a little experience, and a desire to do in wood what those potters were doing in clay. "Today I wrestle with laminate color combinations, finish, and final forms," he says.

A full-time woodworker since 1977, Thomas now lives with his own family on a ridge above Weston a few hundred yards from the farmhouse where his father and grandfather were born.

Rolling Pin & French Rolling Pin, dyed New England rock maple veneers sandwiched together, 16" H x 2¼" DIA

Rolling Pins and Candleholders

Construction:
The forms that I turn on a lathe evolve from a three-part process. First, I enjoy full, rounded curves that appear to be containing something, the way water shapes itself when held in cloth.

Second, the shapes are designed to be inconvenient for mass-production and they will contain zigs and zags and clean, sharp lines that duplicating lathes cannot reproduce.

Third, shapes are determined by the nature of the material being turned. The colorwood I use has a high glue content, making it very stable and strong, and it gives me the opportunity to design in crisp edges that will not chip out the way walnut or butternut would. I can also get the pieces very thin consistently. Some of my designs taper to about ⅛" before flaring out to a larger curve. Vertical pieces, be they bowls, candleholders or vases, should have a beginning and an end, a foot and a rim or finial, and I try to balance the positive and negative space.

Turn rolling pins and candleholders according to dimensions provided in diagrams on page 73.

*Candleholders, dyed New England
rock maple veneers sandwiched
together, approximately 3" H and 7" H*

Rolling pins diagrams for page 71.

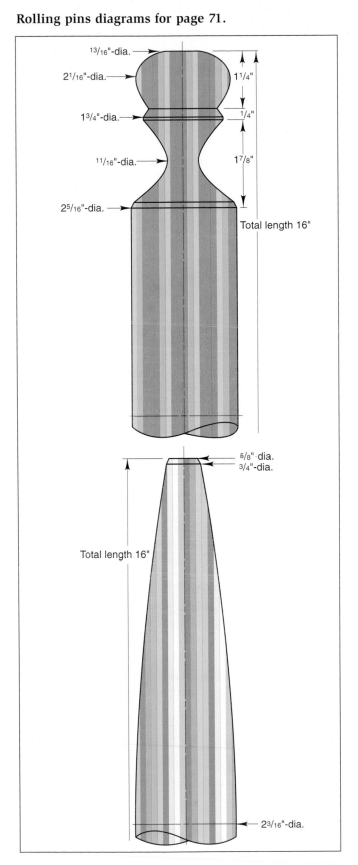

13/16"-dia.

2 1/16"-dia.

1 3/4"-dia.

11/16"-dia.

2 5/16"-dia.

1 1/4"

1/4"

1 7/8"

Total length 16"

5/8"-dia.
3/4"-dia.

Total length 16"

2 3/16"-dia.

Candleholders diagrams for page 71.

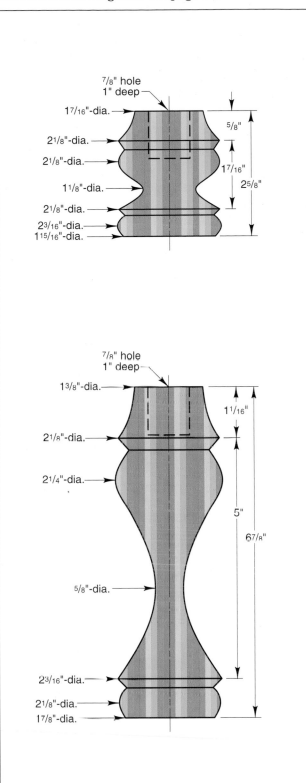

7/8" hole
1" deep

1 7/16"-dia.

2 1/8"-dia.

2 1/8"-dia.

1 1/8"-dia.

2 1/8"-dia.

2 3/16"-dia.
1 15/16"-dia.

5/8"

1 7/16"

2 5/8"

7/8" hole
1" deep

1 3/8"-dia.

2 1/8"-dia.

2 1/4"-dia.

5/8"-dia.

2 3/16"-dia.

2 1/8"-dia.

1 7/8"-dia.

1 1/16"

5"

6 7/8"

Angelo Iafrate

A native Rhode Islander, Angelo Iafrate received a degree in architectural design and drafting from Franklin Institute of Boston. He furthered his studies at the Rhode Island School of Design, The School of the Museum of Fine Arts in Boston and the fine arts school at Rhode Island College. "Through all of the art programs, the most important things to me were color and texture," he says. "I am intrigued with color, seduced by it. It was only natural that these interests would be carried over to my woodworking."

Angelo loved the exotic woods, finding their color and grain too hard to resist. As exotics became less popular because of environmental and ecological concerns, he looked for alternatives. At the 1992 AAW Symposium in Purchase, New York, Angelo stumbled on what he felt was a perfect substitute. Someone was selling the last bit of inventory of Pakkawood from a company that had recently gone out of business. He also learned that Dyamondwood was still being made and could be purchased in large sheets from the manufacturer. Angelo, his father, and his son now produce all of their own diagonal pen blanks from about 25 out of the 40 colors available.

Angelo soon found another excellent material for pen making, Wildwood. Wildwood is a stabilization process that can be used on highly figured wood to help densify and color it. This process has allowed the Iafrates to create turnings from purple big leaf maple burl to chartreuse spalted maple to screaming yellow curly maple—the colors are limited only by the imagination. Angelo selects his material and has it stabilized by Jim Fray of Wildwood. He has expanded the scope of Wildwood from knife handles and pen blanks to include larger turnings, such as bowls and boxes.

Left:
Wildwood
Bowl, spalted
sycamore,
10" DIA, and

Right:
Wildwood
Bowl, spalted
maple, 7" DIA

Candlesticks,
cherry wood,
9⅛" x 5½" DIA
at base

Candlesticks and Bowl

Construction:
Turn candlesticks and bowl according to dimensions provided in the diagrams.

Candlesticks diagram

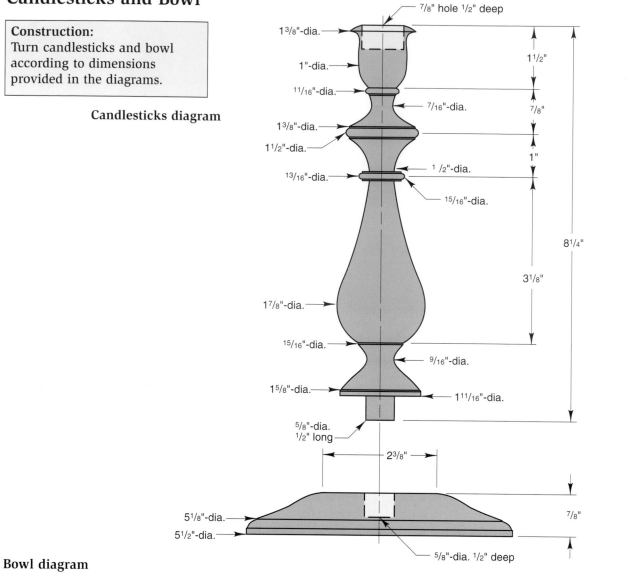

7/8" hole 1/2" deep

1 3/8"-dia.

1"-dia.

11/16"-dia.

7/16"-dia.

1 3/8"-dia.

1 1/2"-dia.

1 /2"-dia.

13/16"-dia.

15/16"-dia.

1 7/8"-dia.

15/16"-dia.

9/16"-dia.

1 5/8"-dia.

1 11/16"-dia.

5/8"-dia. 1/2" long

1 1/2"

7/8"

1"

8 1/4"

3 1/8"

2 3/8"

5 1/8"-dia.

5 1/2"-dia.

7/8"

5/8"-dia. 1/2" deep

Bowl diagram

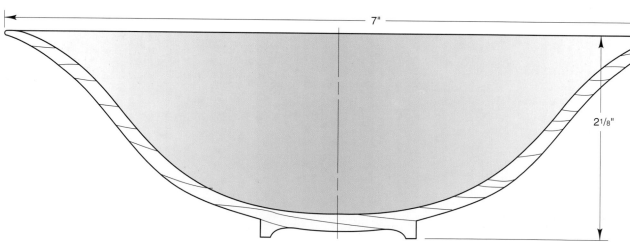

7"

2 1/8"

Frank Luedtke

Frank Luedtke really had no particular interest in woodworking when he came across an old Sears radial arm saw at a garage sale. On a whim, he bought it for $75. One thing led to another and soon he was producing boxes and cutting boards with his partner, Lin Mullins (also pictured), which they sold at flea markets and art fairs.

In 1975, book in one hand, gouge in the other, Frank started turning bowls. "It was slow going and spectacularly unprofitable," he says.

In 1989, Frank and Lin opened Franklin Woods Studio-Gallery in Door County, Wisconsin, and have since turned thousands of vases, lamps and pens. Unlike other turners, Luedtke rarely does "one of" x-number museum pieces, choosing, instead, production spindle turning. "It allows me to practice tool technique and refine my shapes," Frank says. "It's profitable for me and allows my customers to take home an affordable, handmade souvenir from Door County."

The bulk of his turning is done on an old 12" x 36" Walker Turner lathe, using a 1½" roughing gouge, a ½" skew, a ½" spindle gouge, and his favorite little ¼" bowl gouge. "I draw inspiration for turned shapes (and life in general) from the female form and classical Roman and Grecian potters," he says. "The 'perfect' form remains an elusive goal. Possibly after turning a few thousand more pieces, I'll find it."

Above: Bottle Stoppers, various woods

Left: Medium Textured Vase, 8½" H x 3½" DIA, and Small Textured Vase, 4" H x 3¼" DIA

Raffia Vase, beech with raffia wrap and hanging ornaments, 13¾" H x 4½" DIA

Clockwise from left: Perfume Bottle 1, all cocobolo base and Pakkawood (resin-impregnated veneers) stem/cap, multicolored spacer is actually a chip of layers of paint removed from spray booth, 6¾" H x 1¾" DIA (see diagram on page 80); Perfume Bottle 2, base of cocobolo with some chatter work around the top, the stem/cap of the bottle is a built-up lamination of various materials, including Pakkawood (various colored veneers), cocobolo, spacer material, and Corian, 6¼" H x 1¾" DIA (no diagram); Perfume Bottle 3, base is cocobolo as is lower section of stem/cap with plastic spacer material and chechen top, 1¾" DIA x 6⅛" H (see diagram on page 80; Miniature Vessel by Angelo Iafrate, Dyamond wood with a Zacchaelis nut cap

Small Textured Vase (photo on page 77)

Description:
3¼" diameter x 4" high.

Construction:
Turn vase according to dimensions provided in the diagram on page 80. When turning is complete, plug hole. Finish with clear base coat and two coats of amber crackle aerosol spray finish.

Medium Textured Vase (photo on page 77)

Description:
3½" diameter x 8½" high.

Construction:
Turn vase according to dimensions provided in the description. When turning is complete, plug hole. Finish with undercoat of solid blue and two coats of black crackle and some amber aerosol spray finish.

Bottle Stoppers (photo on page 77)

Construction:
1. Drill and glue in a length of dowel to prepare the turning blanks (see diagram on page 80).

2. Chuck in Jacobs drill chuck and turn to desired shape and finish.

3. Glue cork (with prebored hole ⅜" in diameter) in place for a completed bottle stopper.

Raffia Vase (photo on page 78)

Description:
4½" diameter x 13¾" high. Solid beech with raffia wrap and hanging ornaments.

Construction:
Turn vase according to dimensions provided in the diagram on page 80. When turning is complete, plug hole. Raffia is available at crafts supply stores. Use the pattern provided or one of your choice for the ornaments.

Perfume Bottles (photo on page 78)

Construction:
1. Using diagrams for Perfume Bottles 1 and 3 on page 80, turn a cylinder with an end sized for mounting in a chuck.

2. Mount base piece in chuck (spigot or other type).

3. Drill hole to appropriate depth (less threads) and proper diameter to receive glass vial.

4. Shape, sand and finish base.

5. Drill for cap in top piece. Then shape, sand and finish.

6. Screw metal or plastic lid to the glass vial, and glue into the stem/cap with epoxy or gap-filling cyanoacrylate adhesive.

7. With same adhesive, glue the glass bottle into the base with the vial lid still attached and glued in the stem/cap.

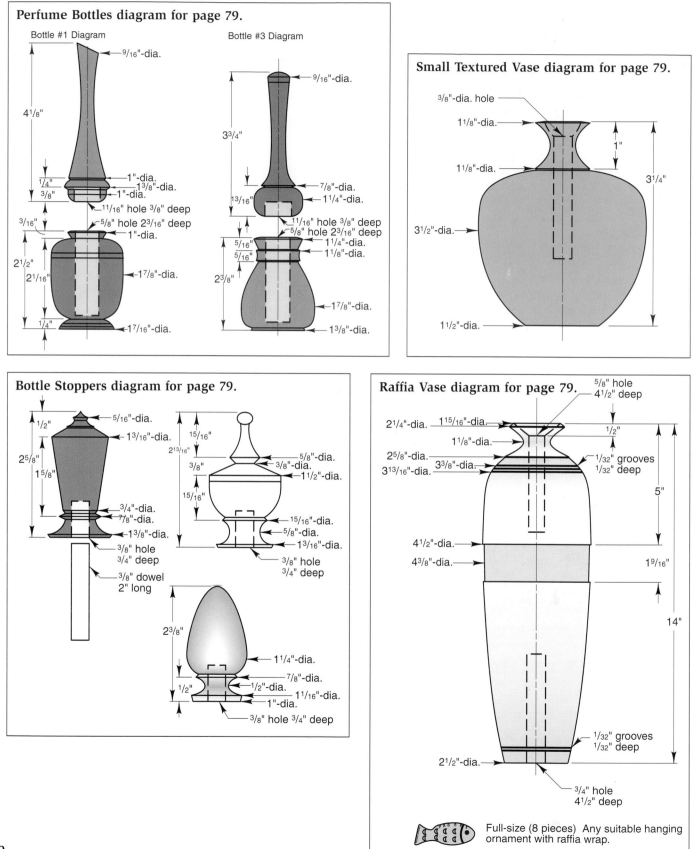

Perfume Bottles diagram for page 79.

Bottle #1 Diagram

Bottle #3 Diagram

9/16"-dia.

9/16"-dia.

4 1/8"

3 3/4"

1/4"
3/8"

1"-dia.
1 3/8"-dia.
1"-dia.
11/16" hole 3/8" deep
5/8" hole 2 3/16" deep
1"-dia.

13/16"

7/8"-dia.
1 1/4"-dia.

11/16" hole 3/8" deep
5/8" hole 2 3/16" deep

3/16"

2 1/2"
2 1/16"

1 7/8"-dia.

1/4"

1 7/16"-dia.

5/16"
5/16"

1 1/4"-dia.
1 1/8"-dia.

2 3/8"

1 7/8"-dia.

1 3/8"-dia.

Small Textured Vase diagram for page 79.

3/8"-dia. hole

1 1/8"-dia.

1"

1 1/8"-dia.

3 1/4"

3 1/2"-dia.

1 1/2"-dia.

Bottle Stoppers diagram for page 79.

5/16"-dia.

1/2"

1 3/16"-dia.

2 5/8"

1 5/8"

15/16"

2 13/16"

3/8"

3/4"-dia.
7/8"-dia.

1 3/8"-dia.

3/8" hole
3/4" deep

3/8" dowel
2" long

5/8"-dia.
3/8"-dia.
1 1/2"-dia.

15/16"

15/16"-dia.
5/8"-dia.
1 3/16"-dia.

3/8" hole
3/4" deep

2 3/8"

1 1/4"-dia.

7/8"-dia.
1/2"-dia.
1 1/16"-dia.
1"-dia.

1/2"

3/8" hole 3/4" deep

Raffia Vase diagram for page 79.

5/8" hole
4 1/2" deep

2 1/4"-dia.
1 15/16"-dia.
1 1/8"-dia.
2 5/8"-dia.
3 13/16"-dia.
3 3/8"-dia.

1/2"

1/32" grooves
1/32" deep

5"

4 1/2"-dia.
4 3/8"-dia.

1 9/16"

14"

1/32" grooves
1/32" deep

2 1/2"-dia.

3/4" hole
4 1/2" deep

Full-size (8 pieces) Any suitable hanging ornament with raffia wrap.

Mark Morrison

Mark Morrison was born in Ogden, Utah, in 1944 and was raised in a Navy family, living up and down the length of both coasts and in Japan and Puerto Rico. After serving his own "hitch" in the Navy, he traveled and worked odd jobs for several years, finally settling in Madison, Wisconsin, in 1968.

By the time he started art school in 1974, he was a published cartoonist and had done an album cover for the rock band, Circus.

After graduating from art school, he worked as a commercial artist, and, in his spare time, he began painting landscapes. As his paintings were accepted by juried shows, he found he needed to make his own frames to get the quality he desired. He learned how to make moldings from hardwood and how to combine moldings for extra-rich effects. Mark's interest in woodworking grew and his woodshop expanded.

In 1992, Mark bought his first lathe because he needed to turn two small parts for an item he was going do as a production run. "Within a matter of days thoughts of doing anything but turning were gone," he says. "I never made that item.

"Woodturning is the perfect combination of fine woods, designing and working with my hands. My work is starting to appear in galleries in the Midwest and I'm looking forward to many years of perfecting my skills and developing my style."

Currently, Mark resides in the tiny rural village of Mt. Hope, Wisconsin.

White on Black Bowl (photo on page 82)

Construction:
1. Glue a round waste block to the bowl blank then turn it with the block mounted in a Nova chuck.

2. Use tailstock for support while the outside is formed.

3. Remove the tailstock and hollow the bowl.

4. Ebonize the bowl inside and out with black aniline dye and allow it to dry.

5. Finish the bowl inside and out with padding lacquer. Part it off the lathe.

6. The pedestal rim on the bottom of the bowl can be formed by making a false jaw set for the Nova Cole Jaws that will expand into the bowl rim, allowing the bottom to be turned.

7. Turn the lid on a small screw chuck, shaping the inside, concave surface first. Then reverse the stock to turn the outside.

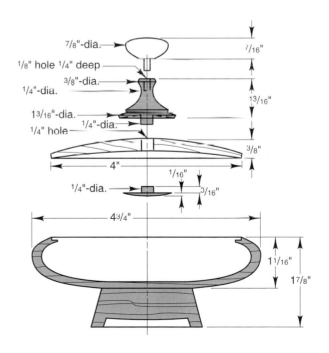

White on Black Bowl, ebonized walnut and curly maple, 3⁷⁄₁₆" H x 4¾" DIA

Ornaments, walnut, basswood and mahogany, 5½" H x 2" DIA

Ornaments

Construction:
Ornaments alternate walnut, basswood and mahogany woods. All ornaments are variations on these methods of glued assembly.

1. Turn the two heart-shaped components by drilling the mahogany billets, then jam-fitting them onto spigots.

2. Finish on the lathe with padding lacquer tinted with red aniline dye.

Ornaments diagrams

Screw eye
$3/4$"-dia.
$1/2$"-dia.
$11/16$"-dia.
$1 1/16$"-dia.
$1/4$"-dia.
$3/4$"

$15/16$"
$1 15/16$"-dia.
$1/4$" hole

$1/2$"
$7/8$"-dia.
$1/2$"-dia.
$1 3/8$"
$3 7/8$"
$13/16$"
$3/8$"-dia.
$7/16$"-dia.
$5/16$"-dia.
$13/16$"

Screw eye
$5/16$"
$9/16$"-dia.
$11/16$"
1"-dia.
$1/4$"-dia.
$11/16$"
2"-dia.
$1/4$" hole

$1/4$"-dia.
$7/8$"-dia.
$7/16$"
$7/8$"-dia.
$1 3/8$"
$2 13/16$"
$1/4$"-dia.
$11/16$"

Screw eye
$3/16$"-dia.
$11/16$"
$1/8$"-dia.
$11/16$"
$7/8$"-dia.
$1/8$" hole

$1/8$"-dia.
$5/8$"-dia.
$2 1/16$"
$2 3/8$"
$1 1/8$"-dia.
$1/4$" hole $1/4$" deep
$1 1/4$"
2"-dia.

83

Robert Rosand

Woodturner Robert Rosand has a degree in psychology and completed two years of graduate work at the University of North Carolina at Greensboro. His love for woodworking led him to carpentry and fine cabinet-making, and articles in woodturning magazines drew his attention to the lathe. His 15 years at perfecting his craft has earned him a style of his own in the woodturning world.

In the last few years, Robert has devoted some of his time to writing articles on woodturning, which appear regularly in *American Woodworker* and *American Woodturner*, where he is also the page editor for "Turning Tips."

Robert is a member of the Pennsylvania Guild of Craftsmen and the American Craft Association and a founding member of the American Association of Woodturners. His works are in private collections throughout the United States and Europe, and his recent awards include the Steinman Center Award, "Best Collaboration" at the State Craft Festival, Lancaster, Pennsylvania, and first and second prize at the Yellow Springs Craft Gallery sponsored by the Pennsylvania Guild. A turning was recently accepted by "Woodturning: Vision and Concept ll," at the Arrowmont School in Gatlinburg, Tennessee. His birdhouses and birdhouse ornaments have consistently won awards at the Vita birdhouse competition in Doylestown, Pennsylvania. From 1991 to 1994, Robert was recognized by the board of the AAW for outstanding contribution to the field of woodturning.

Robert lives with his wife, Susan, and four cats in a house that he built in the woods of Pennsylvania.

Tree Topper, maple burl and walnut, 9" H x 2½" DIA

Birdhouse Ornaments, various woods including walnut, maple, ash, maple burl, walnut burl, and ebony, 6¾" H x 3" DIA

Three-Footed Bowl, 1⅞" H x 5⅝" DIA

Tree Topper (photo on page 84)

The overall height is about 9" with a diameter of 2½". Burl is used for the globe, and walnut, maple or cherry for the icicle or finial. The globe is hollow-turned to about ⅛", and a "funnel" on the bottom allows it to be fit to the top of a tree. The finial and the "funnel" are made of two separate pieces of stock, 1½" square, one about 6½" long, the other about 2" long. Both pieces are turned to a cylinder prior to being held and turned in a three-jaw chuck.

Construction:

1. Glue stock to be used for the globe portion to a waste block which is fastened to a faceplate or that is held by a three-jaw chuck.

2. Turn the globe, leaving enough material at the base to allow hollowing and final turning.

3. Drill a ⅜" hole through the entire globe to mark the top of the ornament and to begin the hollowing procedure.

4. Widen the hole at the base to about ¾". (This is also the area of the globe that will receive the funnel.)

5. Hollow the globe, using a variety of bent-angle and straight-shafted turning tools.

6. Refine the top of the globe; then sand and part off the lathe.

7. Begin the finial and funnel by holding the 6½" piece of wood in the three-jaw chuck. Turn top segment, sand and finish it before proceeding to the next segment, which is subsequently turned, sanded and finished before proceeding to the next, and so on. Turn four segments in this manner, trying to make each a bit larger and longer than the previous. (This method is used because of the tendency of the wood to warp and move on occasion. Rather than try to go back and sand a finial that is wobbling, finish it immediately. If the wobble is too great, discard the piece and begin again.)

8. Turn the bottom section of the finial with a variety of gouges and skews for a variety of forms.

9. When turning is complete, fit the finial to the ⅜" hole in the globe. Undercut the finial at its base until you have a ⅜" tenon. Part off and glue to the globe.

10. Holding the 2" piece of stock for the funnel in the three-jaw chuck, drill a ½" hole entirely through it.

11. With a small gouge, open the hole a bit to fit on the top of a tree. Turn and refine the outer shape of this funnel.

12. When satisfied with the shape, turn a tenon to fit the ¾" hole, making certain to undercut and ensure a tight fit.

13. Glue the funnel in place. Allow to dry and spray ornament with Deft semi-gloss lacquer.

Tree Topper diagram

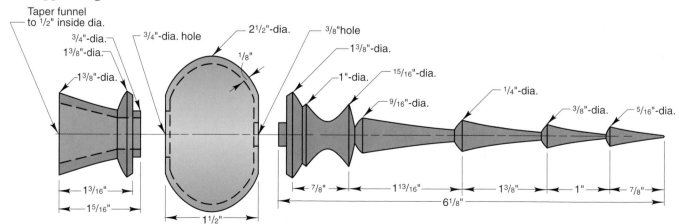

Birdhouse Ornaments (photo on page 85)

The body of the birdhouse is usually made of some straight-grained wood, such as walnut, maple or ash. The roof and bottom are generally made of burl, such as maple or walnut, and the finial, perch and acorn finial are of a contrasting wood, such as ebony.

Construction:

1. For the body, use a piece of wood approximately 1⅝" square by about 4" long. Before turning, center and drill a ½" hole for the entrance and about a 1/16" hole for the perch.

2. Holding the block in a three-jaw chuck, turn to a cylinder.

3. Drill a hole through the center. Using a small round-nosed and square-ended scraper, remove the interior, leaving a wall thickness of about 3/32".

4. Sand the exterior and part off at the appropriate length.

5. For the roof, glue chosen stock to the waste block, allowing enough width for the overhang of the roof and enough length for some waste to be left over for the bottom of the birdhouse.

6. True-up the stock and turn the interior of the birdhouse roof, cutting a small rabbet for the birdhouse body to fit in.

7. Bring up the tailstock for support and turn the remainder of the roof. Sand and carefully part off the roof.

8. Reverse the roof and friction-fit it in a scrap block. (This allows for drilling a small hole in the top, which will later accept the finial.)

9. With the remaining stock, turn the bottom of the birdhouse.

10. Drill a hole, which will later receive the acorn finial. Part off the birdhouse from the waste block.

11. Glue the roof and bottom to the body.

12. With contrasting wood, turn the perch to appropriate size and glue in place.

13. Before turning finial, drill a hole for inserting a #217 ½" brass screw eye for hanging. Turn finial and acorn finial to about ⅜" finished diameter, allowing for tenons attaching to birdhouse. Glue to birdhouse.

14. Insert brass screw eye. Allow to dry and finish-spray with Deft semi-gloss lacquer.

Birdhouse Ornaments diagram

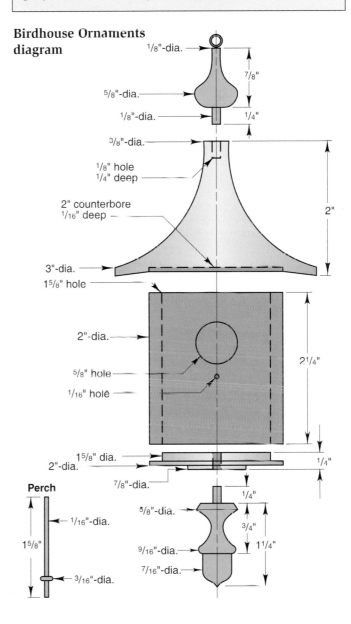

Perch

87

Three-Footed Bowl (photo on page 85)

Turned bowls have been around for some time, but it was an article by Rodger Jacobs of North Carolina that spurred me on to attempting the style of bowl featured here. The technique for making these bowls is not all that different from the creation of a "regular" bowl with the addition of the carved feet, but the visual effect of the footed bowl can be stunning.

Construction:

1. Glue turning stock to waste block fastened to faceplate. True-up the sides and top of the block and then begin to shape the exterior of the bowl, leaving enough material at the foot of the bowl to avoid chatter when hollowing the interior. Turn the inside of the bowl.

2. Return to the bottom of the bowl and refine the shape.

3. Sand and finish both inside and out. Remove bowl from waste block with a band saw or parting tool.

4. Measure the bottom of the bowl to determine how deep the feet will be. (The finished bottom should be the same thickness as the wall sides or the visual effect will be heavy.)

5. Friction-fit the top of the bowl into a block of scrap wood that has been fastened to a faceplate. Turn the bottom out of the bowl. Wall consistency is important.

6. Leaving the bowl in the fiction-fit chuck, mark out the location of the feet with a paper gauge that has been divided into thirds. Also mark out the profile of the feet with another paper gauge.

7. Rough-cut around the feet with a coping saw, and begin removing all the excess material between the feet with a rotary rasp in a die grinder.

8. Use a small drum sander for rough sanding. Finalize and refine the shape of the bowl with foam-backed sanding discs of various sizes, depending on the size of the bowl.

9. Remove the bowl from the friction-fit chuck and finish with Waterlox.

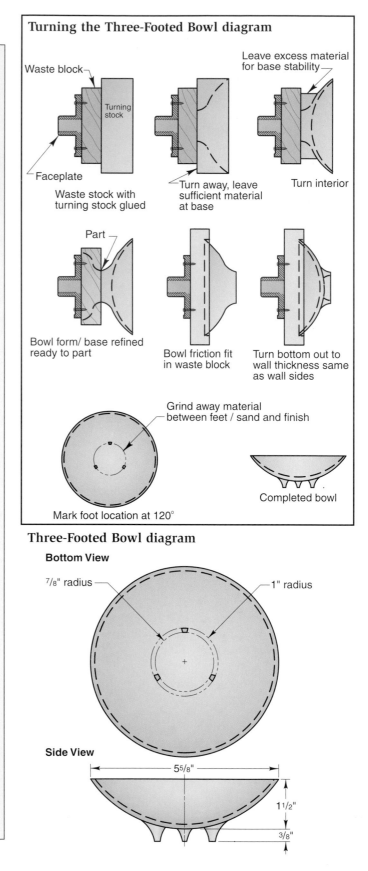

Turning the Three-Footed Bowl diagram

Waste block

Turning stock

Faceplate

Waste stock with turning stock glued

Turn away, leave sufficient material at base

Leave excess material for base stability

Turn interior

Part

Bowl form/ base refined ready to part

Bowl friction fit in waste block

Turn bottom out to wall thickness same as wall sides

Grind away material between feet / sand and finish

Mark foot location at 120°

Completed bowl

Three-Footed Bowl diagram

Bottom View

7/8" radius

1" radius

Side View

5 5/8"

1 1/2"

3/8"

Nathan Roth

In the fall of 1938 as a sophomore at Monroe High School, in Monroe, Wisconsin, Nathan Roth turned his first bowl in birch. Since then, he has turned hundreds, maybe thousands, of pieces. Along with antique restoring, Nathan does a considerable amount of architectural turning: spindles, table legs and finials. One of his favorite jobs was turning parts for an antique spinning wheel which was made in 1791.

Nathan is excited to see a renaissance of the craft. "The lathe can be one of the most creative machines in the workshop," he says. "It is all up to the turner. It takes a lot of patience and practice to learn and perfect your techniques. After 56 years of turning, I am still learning!"

Chess set, ebony and maple, pieces range from 1¼" to 2¼" H

Chess

Construction: Turn and carve chess pieces according to full-size diagrams below.

Knight, Front View

Knight, Side View

Knight, Back View

Bishop

Pawn

King

Queen, with Top View

Rook, with Top View

90

Betty Scarpino

photo by Tom Casalini

"Working with wood—and all that it involves—is a wonderful vehicle for my journeys in life," says Betty Scarpino. She took her very first woodworking class 17 years ago and discovered that the combination of working with her hands and with wood felt quite comfortable. In the years that followed, with woodworking as a focus, Betty learned that she also enjoyed teaching and demonstrating.

Betty's teaching and demonstrating has included numerous trips to Canada for turning demonstrations, teaching woodturning at the Appalachian Center for Crafts in Tennessee, and three summers teaching a one-week beginning woodworking class at the WoodenBoat School in Maine. She edited *American Woodturner*, journal of the American Association of Woodturners, for three years and was a consultant for *The Art of Woodworking: Wood Turning*, a Time-Life book published in 1994.

While enrolled as an industrial arts student, Betty took several fine arts classes, including sculpture. "My work is beginning to reflect what has been a continued interest and fascination with sculpture, so it seems quite natural to use the lathe as one of the many tools in the process of creating with wood," she says. "I have started to carve, cut up, bleach, and texture my turnings. I am not sure where my working with wood will take me in the years to come, but I do know that with wood as the vehicle, the journey will be full of adventure."

Walnut Platter (photo on page 92)

Construction:
Turn plate and stand according to dimensions provided in the diagram.

Bleaching and carving a section of a walnut piece gives the same visual effect as inlaying. A raised section of the plate is cut with grooves. After the piece is finished and off the lathe, that part is carefully bleached twice, using a cotton-tipped swab. Carve through the grooves, then use a woodburner to darken the carving marks and add other design markings.

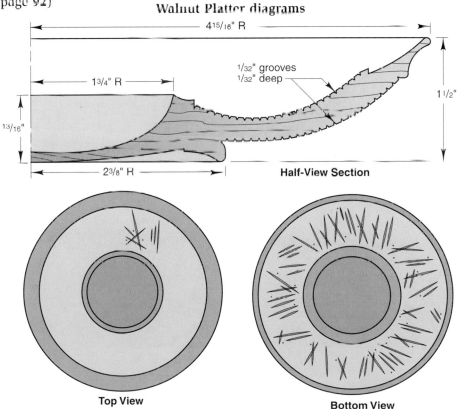

Walnut Platter diagrams

Half-View Section

Top View

Bottom View

*Walnut Platter, walnut bleached and
carved, 1½" H x 9⅞" DIA*

Bleached Plate and Stand, hard maple, 1½" H x 12" DIA

Two-Piece Birdhouse, turned in the same fashion as a lidded box; Turned Tops, maple and walnut, 1⅞" H x 1⅞" DIA; Egg, a popular collectible

Left: Osage Orange Bowl, bleached and with beads, 3¾" H x 6" DIA

Right: Silver Maple Bowl, bleached and grooved

Bleached Plate and Stand (photo on page 93)

Plates are wonderful turned items to decorate and make a bold statement when placed in a stand created to work with the design of the plate. This plate and stand are made from hard maple.

Construction:

1. Turn the plate as you would any faceplate work.

2. Sand and part off the lathe.

3. Using a soft pencil, draw edge designs on the plate.

4. When you are satisfied with the designs, make the cuts with a band saw, jigsaw, or a hand-held saw. (If you use power equipment to make the cuts, be sure that the plate rests firmly on the table of the machine.)

5. Use a wood file to clean up the rough cuts. Progress to abrasive paper, and finish up with at least 220-grit or finer paper, making minor adjustments in the edges as necessary.

6. Bleach and texture portions of the plate as desired.

7. Use two or three leftover pieces of wood to make the stand. Select a piece large and heavy enough to hold the plate firmly. Begin shaping the piece on a band saw or belt sander.

8. Carve a groove to hold the plate upright. The groove needs to be slanted at the angle that you want the plate to be presented.

Bleached Plate diagram

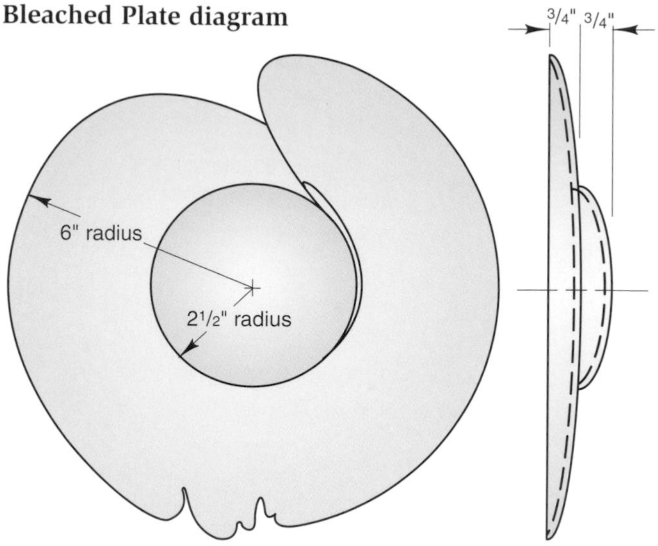

6" radius

2½" radius

3/4" 3/4"

Bleached Plate Stand diagram

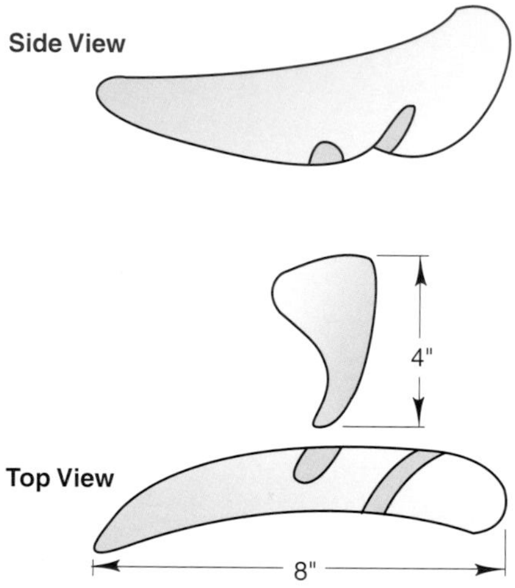

Side View

Top View

4"

8"

Bleached Plate and Stand, reverse angle

Two-Piece Birdhouse (photo on page 93)

These birdhouses are turned in the same fashion that a lidded box is turned. It makes for a simple two-part turning which is relatively easy to accomplish. The birdhouses can be hung as decorations all year-round.

Construction:

1. Attach a 5" long x 1¾" thick piece of wood to the lathe either in a chuck or by gluing one end to a faceplate with an auxiliary block screwed to it. Use thick cyanoacrylate glue for end-grain gluing in this fashion.

2. Rough out the outside shape of the cylinder for the body of the birdhouse, marking where the roof will begin.

3. Turn off the lathe, then drill an entrance hole approximately ¼" deep into the side of the cylinder, slightly above center.

4. Hollow out the inside of the birdhouse, taking care not to cut too deeply where the roof will slant inward.

5. Return to the outside of the birdhouse, and turn the roof section until attached by only a small portion of wood.

6. Remove the tool rest and sand as necessary.

7. Part off the birdhouse at the tip of the roof, and clean up the tip of the roof with a bit of sandpaper.

8. With the remaining wood, turn the bottom of the birdhouse, using the hollowed-out section as a gauge for a good fit. (It does not have to fit snugly like a lidded box because the pieces will be glued together.) Slightly hollow out the bottom section.

9. Sand as necessary and part off the lathe.

10. Glue the pieces together, then add a perch as desired. (A small section of a round toothpick works great to stick into a small predrilled hole.)

11. Add a small eye hook for hanging, and finish as desired.

Two-Piece Birdhouse diagram

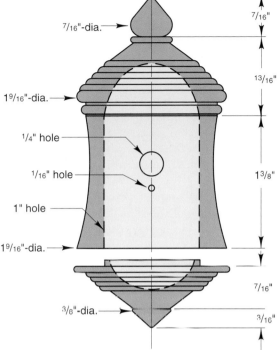

Turning the Two-Piece Birdhouse diagram

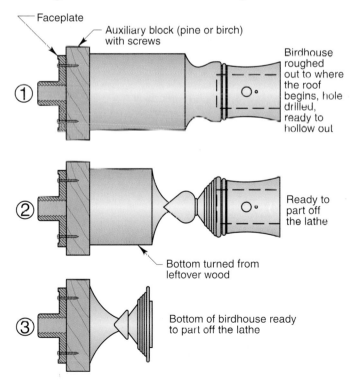

① Birdhouse roughed out to where the roof begins, hole drilled, ready to hollow out

② Ready to part off the lathe

Bottom turned from leftover wood

③ Bottom of birdhouse ready to part off the lathe

Turned Tops (photo on page 93)

Construction:

1. Cut a 4" length of 1¾"-thick stock. (This is enough wood to make two tops.) Glue one end to a waste block attached to a faceplate using cyanoacrylate adhesive.

2. Turn tops with the stem first to easily include a bit of turned detail on the top side as the design calls for it. (Turning in this fashion, however, means that particular care needs to be given to how the top is parted off at the tip. Otherwise, the tip where the top spins will have a small hole torn in it.)

3. Make the final parting cut with a skew, cutting on the waste block side of the top. (There will be a bit of extra wood attached to the tip, but that is quickly and easily removed using the skew as a knife.)

4. Use a handheld reciprocating carver for carving the decorations, being careful to keep your fingers away from the path of the carver.

5. For colored tops, paint as desired with watercolor paints in tubes purchased at crafts stores.

6. To speed this part of the process, apply a coat of lacquer to the top before carving and carve through the lacquer. (The watercolor paint will stick to the unfinished carved portion and can easily be removed from the uncarved area by rubbing with fine steel wool.)

7. To decorate the walnut top with the turned grooves and carving, apply two coats of bleach to the grooved area with a cotton-tipped swab.

8. After bleaching, carve through the bleached grooves and use a woodburner to highlight the carvings.

9. Finish as desired.

Tops diagrams

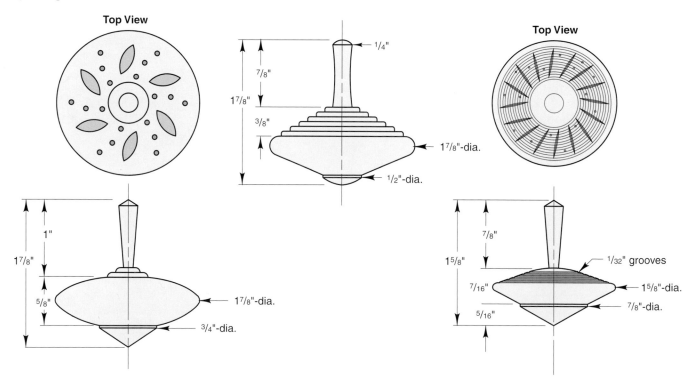

96

Bleached Bowls (photo on page 93)

Use a two-part liquid wood bleach that is available locally at large lumber stores. Follow the directions on the box. Use eye protection and gloves, and do not breathe the fumes.

The results of bleaching different types of wood are as varied as wood itself. Maple bleaches well with two or three bleachings. Occasionally bleach will turn a piece a yellowish or orange color, so if you are not sure about the reaction of a particular type of wood to bleach, try bleaching a cut-off section of the wood first.

Some woods tend to crack and split in the end grain part if bleached more than two or three times.

Almost any finish works well over bleached wood, but any finish will darken the color. The featured walnut pieces are finished first with a coat of Danish oil, then two coats of lacquer. The pieces that are bleached totally white, are not finished further. For maple and other lighter color woods that have only sections of the piece bleached, finish with three coats of lacquer.

Oil, grease, steel wool, finish and other substances react with bleach or inhibit the bleaching process. Handle with care any piece that is being bleached or that has been bleached.

> **Construction:**
> Turn Silver Maple bowl according to dimensions provided in the diagram below.

Silver Maple Bleached Bowl
Silver maple is one of the "soft" maples. Air drying silver maple often results in a grayish color in the wood. By bleaching only the turned-groove section of the bowl, it contrasts nicely with the gray. The bleaching of a section of a turned piece, as a highlight, works well with many other colors and types of wood. It "brings alive" many turned bowls that would otherwise have been visually dull, simply because of the color of the wood.

Osage Orange Bleached Bowl
The color of Osage orange wood is a beautiful, bright yellowish-brown which turns to a mellow, brownish-golden color with exposure to light. There is a marked difference in the early and late growth rings; bleaching Osage orange highlights that difference and gives the finished piece a look similar to that of sandblasted wood. The turned beads accentuate the lines of the growth rings and provide a delightful visual pattern.

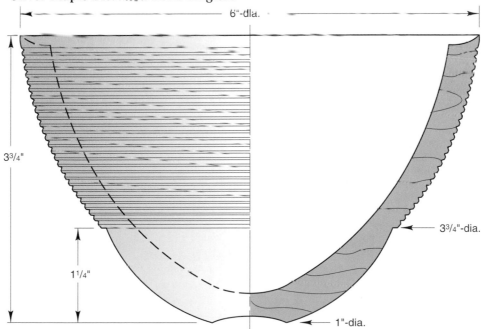

Silver Maple Bleached Bowl diagram

6"-dia.

3³/₄"

1¹/₄"

3³/₄"-dia.

1"-dia.

Dick Sing

Dick Sing was born in 1940 on a farm in Joliet, Illinois. He became a tool and die maker and then worked in quality control for General Motors. When he was offered an early retirement in 1989 because of plant closure, he took it.

Although Dick started turning in 1965, he did not attend his first symposium until 1986. He then began taking classes and attending demonstrations to expand his knowledge of turning. After retiring, his hobby turned into his profession.

Dick conducts instructional demonstrations for clubs, stores, and shows. In 1995, he was invited to be one of the demonstrators at the Utah Wood Turners Conference at Brigham Young University.

Dick is the author of *Woodlathe Projects For Fun And Profit* and *Useful Beauty, Turning Practical Items On A Woodlathe*. He still makes his home in Joliet with his wife, Cindy.

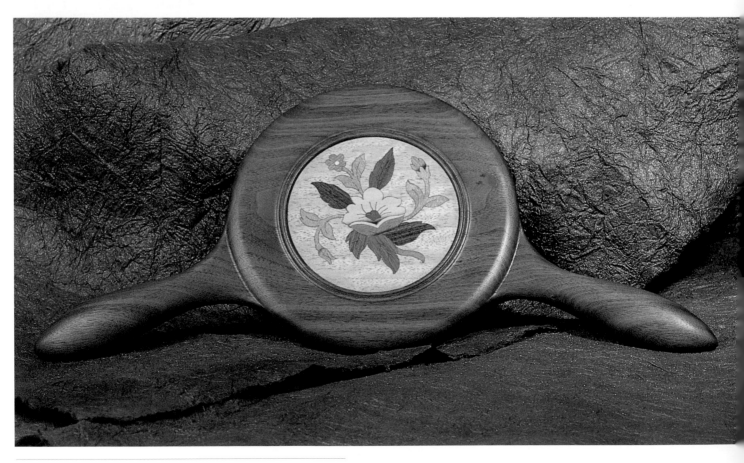

Two-Handled Mirror, walnut with pre-made veneer-marquetry inlay, 15" L x ⅞" x 6⅝" DIA

Two-Handled Mirror

The wood used is a walnut with distinguishing streaking markings to make it obvious that the mirror is made from one piece of wood. Also used is a pre-made marquetry inlay framed with a turned bead and gentle contours to adorn the back.

Sharp tools are a must along with a light-controlled touch. The outside diameter and handles are worked by hand, adding another dimension to the project. Most of the turning can be done with a spindle gouge, and a parting tool or square scraper will help cut a clean recess for the mirror.

Materials:
6"-diameter beveled glass mirror
4"-diameter veneer-marquetry inlay
Wood for the body
Silicone adhesive for gluing in the glass mirror

Construction:
1. Using the diagrams on pages 100 and 101, lay out the outline of the glass mirror on a piece of ¾" to 1" stock that is large enough to accommodate the body and handles.

2. Saw out the mirror's overall profile.

3. Attach a scrap block approximately 3" in diameter to a faceplate or screw chuck and true up the mating or front surface.

4. Select the surface that will be the back of the mirror, position the scrap block centered to the body and glue.

5. Mount the assembly to the lathe and rotate by hand to make sure that the handles clear the lathe bed or other obstructions. (Start with a slow lathe speed, as the handles will be windmilling and out of balance.)

6. Start cutting the recess for the 6" glass mirror using a gouge or tool of your choice. Working carefully, increase the recess diameter until the glass mirror can be inserted. (Allow a small amount of clearance around the mirror for wood movement to guard against breakage.)

7. Form a decorative bead around the glass mirror. This bead will start to contact the handles and determine their thickness. Stop often to check your progress.

8. When the bead is formed, insert the glass mirror to make sure the recess is deep enough so that the glass mirror's surface is below the bead. (This is to guard against damage when the mirror is laid face down.)

9. Start to shape the thickness of the handles. Create a pleasing transition from the bead to the handle. (Keep in mind that the other side of the body and handles will also be turned.)

10. Cut clean and finish-sand for a finished surface on the bead and transition.

11. Take off the lathe and remove the faceplate or screw chuck from the scrap block.

12. Mount another piece of scrap on the faceplate or screw chuck. (This must be larger than the recess to create a jam-fit chuck inside the recess.)

13. Carefully reduce the scrap block diameter until it fits snugly inside the recess. (This will center the mirror body and provide a means to drive it.)

14. When a snug drive fit is attained, attach strips of double-face tape to the bottom of the recess and press onto the jam-fit chuck. (This will provide additional holding strength, while allowing removal of the mirror body when finished.)

15. Turn off the scrap block which was glued on the back of the mirror.

16. Start to shape the outside diameter to match the finished bead on the front. (Part of the outside diameter will have to be worked by hand later, as the handles will not allow otherwise.)

17. Make the transition from the body to the handles, establishing their thickness and shape. (By establishing the outside diameter and handle transitions first, it is easier to judge proportions for the inlay and decoration.)

18. Glue veneer-marquetry inlay to a ⅛"-thick backing of scrap. True-up for a precise fit between the inlay and mirror body.

19. Using a trued-up scrap block, attach the inlay with double-face tape.

20. Turn the diameter to the desired dimension, and clean up the face for a glue surface. When the inlay is prepared, remove from the scrap block.

21. Start to turn a recess to accept the prepared inlay. (Keep in mind that there is a mirror recess on the other side.) Carefully increase the recess diameter until the inlay can be inserted. When using a veneered inlay, the depth of the recess is more critical than a solid inlay, as the face cannot be altered for lack of material.

22. Create a small bead around the inlay recess, and contour the back of the mirror to a pleasing shape.

23. Glue in the inlay using the tailstock and a piece of scrap to apply clamping pressure.

24. When the glue has cured, sand the turned portion of the mirror body and inlay.

25. Remove the mirror from the chuck by steadily applying pressure away from the joint until the tape relaxes its grip.

26. Hand-shape the handles using rasps, knives or tool of your choice. Blend the front and rear outside diameters and the transitions to the handles with pleasing contours.

27. When the shaping is complete, sand the entire mirror, checking for flaws or scratches.

28. Apply a liberal coat of an oil finish of your choice. Be sure to finish the mirror's recess to seal against moisture and prevent excessive wood movement. Apply additional coats of oil until the desired finish is achieved.

29. Install the glass mirror into the recess, using silicone adhesive, as it will remain pliable and protect against glass breakage if the mirror body should warp.

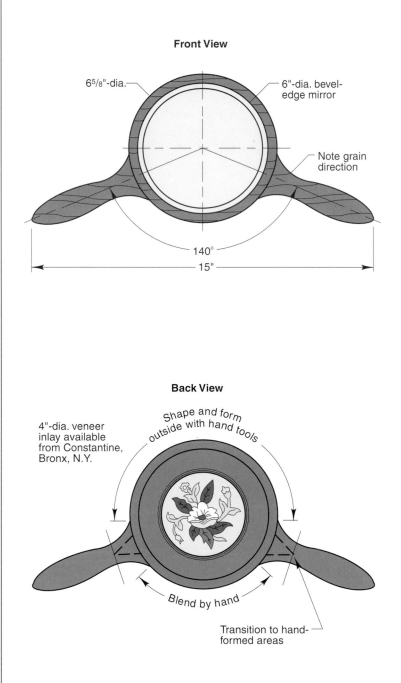

Two-Handled Mirror diagram

Front View

6⅝"-dia.

6"-dia. bevel-edge mirror

Note grain direction

140°

15"

Back View

4"-dia. veneer inlay available from Constantine, Bronx, N.Y.

Shape and form outside with hand tools

Blend by hand

Transition to hand-formed areas

Handle diagrams

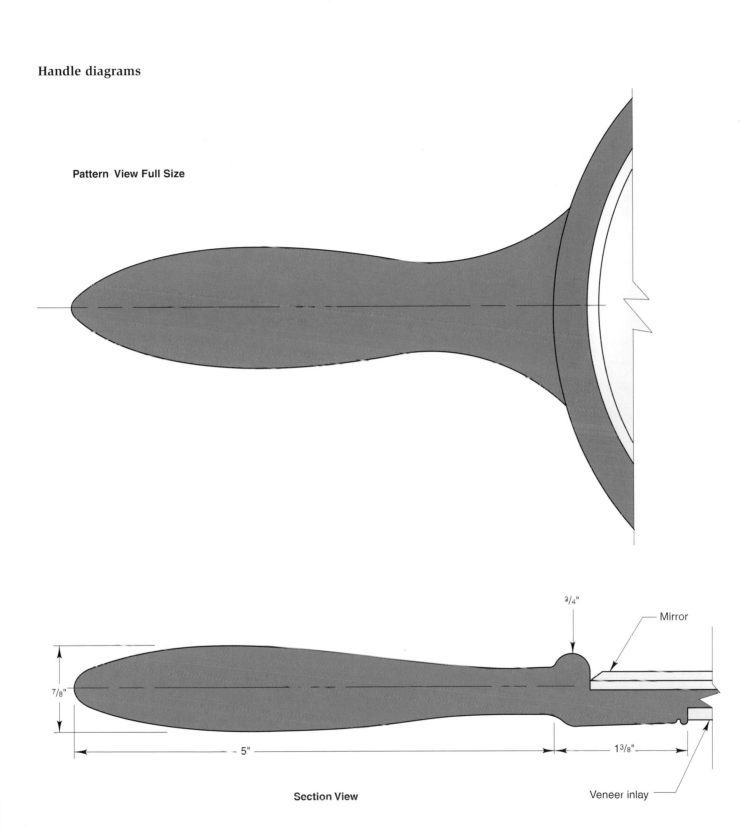

Pattern View Full Size

$^3/_4$"

Mirror

$^7/_8$"

— 5" —

$1^3/_8$"

Section View

Veneer inlay

Artists' Design Concepts & Gallery

Ray Allen

Ray Allen, a self-taught woodturner, creates segmented turnings from his studio in Yuma, Arizona. At 65 years old, Ray works between eight and 12 hours a day, seven days a week, and refers to this work as "a labor of love."

After spending 30 years as a carpenter in the building trade, Ray still felt the need to "construct" something. So he started turning. Living in Arizona, he has been influenced by the southwestern and prehistoric pottery. His works often contain over 3,000 pieces of wood, which are glued and turned, to resemble ancient pottery.

Ray won his first exhibition prize in 1990 and has since been the recipient of many "Best of Show" and first-place awards. His work has been exhibited at such places as the del Mano Gallery in Los Angeles, California, the Highlight Gallery in Mendocino, California, and the Mendelson Gallery in Washington Depot, Connecticut.

Ray's turning on the opposite page contains 3,042 pieces, weighs 35 pounds, stands 26½" tall, and is 30" in diameter. It contains seven kinds of wood: mesquite, satin wood, blood wood, rose wood, curly maple, ebony, and dyed veneer. This piece, along with more than 30 other of his designs, is held in the private collection of Irving Lipton in Van Nuys, California.

"My creations are all put together one piece at a time, starting at the bottom. The segments are cut, sanded, and assembled into rings. Each ring is then turned to the proper diameter and added one at a time. After the piece is completely assembled, it is turned to its final shape and sanded on the outside. The inside is then turned to final wall thickness of ⅛" to 3/16" for 8"-10" pots, and ¼" to ⅜" for the very large pieces, such as the piece shown."

"I am inspired by southwest and prehistoric pottery. The challenge of intricate design and how to construct it gives me the challenge I need. The finished piece gives me the self-satisfaction I enjoy so much."

Held in the Irving Lipton private collection, this turning contains 3,042 pieces of wood and weighs 35 pounds.

Brenda Behrens

Years before Brenda Behrens started turning magnificent bowls on her lathe, she studied woodcarving in Japan under the Japanese woodcarver, Gingi Ishihara. She spent two years learning the basics of tool technique and understanding the importance of keeping your tools sharp. After returning to the United States, she discovered the California Carvers Guild and became a very active member.

Brenda's first experience with the lathe left her neither excited nor inspired. Her secondhand 1930s Sears Craftsman lathe was left to collect dust in the corner of the garage. Five years later, after attending a woodturning symposium, Brenda encountered a world of artistic turning she hadn't known existed. Thus began her quest to combine her woodcarving talents with turned art.

Brenda's work has been exhibited in major galleries throughout California, and she's received such recent honors as having a Christmas tree ornament in the White House and receiving first-place woodturning awards in 1992, 1993 and 1994 at the Southern California Exposition "Design in Wood." She has been featured in radio, TV and magazines, making three appearances in the publication, *American Woodturner*.

Olive Swirl, olive wood, 5¼" H x 8¼" DIA with turquoise nuggets

Garden Rythm, English elm, 7" H x 5¼" DIA

Kip Christensen

Kip Christensen is a professor of Technology Education at Brigham Young University. His primary teaching areas are furniture design and construction, manufacturing, and residential drafting. His teaching experience also includes two years at Humboldt State University in Arcata, California. Kip and his wife, Kim, have five children and live in Springville, Utah.

Kip's first exposure to woodworking came at age 14 while working after school and in the summer at his father's cabinet factory. Later, while an undergraduate student at Brigham Young University, he was introduced to woodturning by Dale Nish. As a student, Kip was particularly inspired and motivated by teachers who not only taught within their chosen discipline, but also produced works relative to the subjects they taught. It has been Kip's goal to provide similar inspiration for his students by continuing to be a producing artisan. As a result of this goal, he has become an accomplished and well-known woodworker. His work has been published in several books, magazines, and woodworking catalogues and displayed in several galleries and art shows. He has been an invited presenter for numerous workshops and symposia.

While Kip is best known for his lidded containers, he also makes bowls, vessels and spindles. His work is characterized by clean lines and fine detail.

Inlaid Lidded Container, the container is of tulipwood, with a border inlay of purpleheart with some chatterwork, and a primary inlay of pink box elder burl

*Right and
below: Antler
Bowls, varying
sizes of bowls
turned from
antler*

Gene Ðoren

Gene Doren was born in Dayton, Ohio, in 1940. After completing high school, he served two years with the Army's 101st Airborne division. Currently, he is an instrument and control technician for Electric Utility in Alaska. Although he worked with wood a bit in high school and here and there through the years, he began woodturning in 1987.

Gene's work is shown in galleries from Alaska to Hawaii, and he has shared his experience at demonstrations for the Alaska Creative Woodworkers Association as well as the Utah Woodturning Symposium at Brigham Young University in 1993.

Most of Gene's pieces are made from Alaska Paper Birch burls that he harvests with the help of some good friends. The burls are green and can range in weight from 1 pound to 1,500 pounds. They are rough-turned while they are still wet and left considerably thicker than the finished product. This compensates for the warping and the movement of the wood during the drying process. After rough turning, the piece is coated inside and out with paste wax and placed in an unheated room for two months. It is then moved to normal room temperature for at least four more months. When dry, the piece is turned "round" again. The piece is sanded in progressively finer grits, from 80 to 600 grit, and then several coats of finish are applied, usually natural Watco oil. Gene finishes the piece with a coat of paste wax.

He has also started creating turnings from palm nuts. The Ivory Nut Palm seed from the South Pacific is a great source of vegetable ivory. It is horseshoe shaped in vertical section, with a large cavity at one end and a small embryo cavity at the other end. "I drill a hole from the small cavity through to the large cavity and then hand-ream the hole with a taper pin reamer. I then glue a fitted taper plug (cut from a second nut or exotic wood) into the hole." These turnings are about 2" wide by 1½" tall.

Large fluted bowl, spalted Alaska paper birch burl, 8" H x 17½" DIA with 189 flutes
"The normal care of the wood is simple, a thin coat of paste wax, rubbed in well and allowed to dull, then buffed with a soft cloth."

Vase, mango, purpleheart, curly walnut, maple and koa, 19" H x 10½" DIA with 120 flutes

Ivory nut turnings, ivory nut palm nuts, African blackwood, approximate size is 1¾" DIA

Small fluted bowl, spalted Alaska paper birch burl, 8" H x 10" DIA with fluting

Melvyn Firmager

Melvyn Firmager is a sculptural woodturner, creating his turnings from his workshop and gallery, Nut Tree Farm, in Wedmore, Somerset, England, since the early 1920s. The beautiful fine wood he was using for heat and cooking rekindled an earlier interest in art—and turning provided a way of expressing the inner beauty and spirit of the wood.

In his early days of turning, he made traditional bowls, platters and candleholders, later experimenting with green wood, making natural-edge bowls, paper-thin vessels and goblets. By 1986, he was turning professionally and, two years later, made his first attempts at hollow-form work. Recently his work has taken a new direction with new and distinctive shapes, including double- and multiple-rim vessels.

On his two acres of land, bed-and-breakfast guests and gallery visitors alike may find Melvyn rummaging through his wood piles to locate a suitable piece for his latest creation. His wood comes mainly from storm-damaged trees.

Melvyn has designed and developed his own tools and special beveled gouges for hollow-form work, which are available to fellow turners. He has also custom-built four lathes with electronic variable-speed controls and remote switching, ideal for bowl and hollow-form work. These lathes are used by his students, whom he teaches from beginner level through to advanced. "I can well remember my own early experiences and feelings of being unsure about even offering a tool to a revolving piece of wood. However, in my courses, even a complete beginner will be using a gouge within minutes of arrival, learning to make smooth and clean cuts. These are exciting moments and indeed great fun."

Melvyn exhibits in many galleries and has given demonstrations at numerous seminars and symposiums throughout Europe and the United States.

Sea Flower, eucalyptus gunnii, 6" H x 5" DIA
"An understanding of how tools cut and how to sharpen them is a major factor in learning to turn. I have developed a technique and gouge bevel which is especially useful for natural edge work, giving greater stability and ease of use."

*Pagoda Vessel,
ebonized eucalyptus,
13" H x 8" DIA
"Deep-fluted gouges
are used with
unusual bevels to
turn deep inside
hollow forms with
small openings, in
both end grain and
across the grain,
which is considerably
superior to using
scrapers."*

*Sea Flower, ebonized eucalyptus, 6" H x 4¾" DIA
"I have developed my own angle tools for reaching
where straight tools cannot go. They have the distinct
advantage over all other angle tools in that they
have a guide which makes them much more stable in
use and reduces the amount of tension required to
control them."*

Ron Fleming

Ron Fleming is a native of Oklahoma. He is a professional illustrator and woodturner, represented in New York, Connecticut, San Francisco, Los Angeles and Philadelphia. He is active in the Art Directors Club of Tulsa (and a past president of that organization), the American Association of Woodturners, and at the Wood Turning Center, where he is currently serving on the board of trustees. He is also a member of the Oklahoma State University - Tech advisory committee.

"I love nature," says Ron. "For many years I watched and helped my father and grandfather work in wood. Observing and learning, thinking and searching for a way to express the feelings and thoughts I have about nature . . . it's beauty and it's passages. Woodturning is a natural way for me to combine my capabilities as an artist and a craftsman.

"Never taking a living tree, but using only 'given' woods, each transformed piece of wood becomes a captured moment in time of it's own existence. Every form gives me a way to express my feelings about the things I see around me and to share these visions with others."

Ron has received many awards for his work, including a 1989 purchase award from the Vision Makers Show, which was sponsored by the State Arts Council of Oklahoma; a purchase award from the 1992 Regional Craft Biennial, sponsored by the Arkansas Arts Center in Little Rock; and the Grand Prize Award in the 1991 American Crafts Awards, which was sponsored by Kraus Sikes, Inc.

photo by Bob Hawks

New Beginnings, redwood burl, 13" H x 19" DIA
(White House permanent collection)

112

*Datura,
basswood with
acrylic paint,
13½" H x 17"
DIA*

*Suspended
Redwood
Flora,
redwood
burl, 21" x
7" H x 12"
W (Irving
Lipton
private
collection)*

Linton Frank

For 30 years Linton Frank made a living in the computer-service industry until major cutbacks left him without a job. Needing to supplement his unemployment, Linton turned to his woodworking hobby as a possible source. Fascinated by the turned objects and forms which he saw in woodturning publications, he enrolled in the David Ellsworth School of Woodturning and got hooked. Shortly thereafter, he purchased a lathe and has been turning ever since.

Linton's style is mostly, but not limited to, hollow forms. "Recently I have been inspired by pottery designs of Southwest Native American tribes, which is evident in my most recent works. The one piece that has inspired me most is the double-spouted wedding vessels made by these tribes. These vessels are used during wedding ceremonies. Water and sacred objects are placed inside the vessel, and the bride and groom each drink from one of the spouts."

The wedding vessel featured here won Linton third place at the amateur division of the *American Woodworker Magazine's* Excellence in Craftsmanship Awards. The vessel is hollowed throughout and turned from broadleaf maple burl on three separate axes. "The wedding-ceremony story behind these vessels inspired me to include that feeling by making the vessel's shape similar to the human heart." The decorative bands on top of the spouts are made from segmented pieces of ebony, maple, and purpleheart, symbolizing the exchange of wedding bands. The ends of the spouts, handle and base are made of ebony. This piece is owned by John Overwise and is exhibited in his gallery, Art For Everyone, in Lansdale, Pennsylvania.

Linton's work has been published in the British magazine *Woodturning,* and his article, "How to Turn a Wedding Vessel," appeared in both the *North Carolina Woodturning Journal* and the American Association of Woodturning's *American Woodturner* June 1994 edition.

Wedding Vessel, broadleaf maple burl, 10½" H x 5½" Deep, decorative bands on top of spouts are made from segmented pieces of ebony, maple and purpleheart; ends of spouts, handle and base are ebony (John Overwise's Art For Everyone gallery collection)

Dewey Garrett

Educated in engineering, Dewey Garrett took up the wood lathe in order to develop general woodworking skills for cabinetry and furniture. He found the process so stimulating and challenging that woodturning has become a dedicated creative pursuit that complements a technical career. He is a self-taught turner and makes and modifies his tools to craft unique turnings. His work is a continuing exploration of the structure of forms constrained by the symmetry and simplicity imparted by the mechanics of a lathe.

Dewey currently exhibits work in local California galleries and shows regularly in national juried competitions for both woodturning and three-dimensional art.

"I am interested in the transformation and contrasts discovered through woodturning," Dewey says. "The process of converting a featureless block of wood into a graceful symmetrical form is always fascinating and full of surprises. While working at the lathe, all the details and colors of the object are integrated into a spinning blur that reveals only its outline. At rest, the same object can disclose complex details and dramatic coloring, while possessing an entirely different sense of motion."

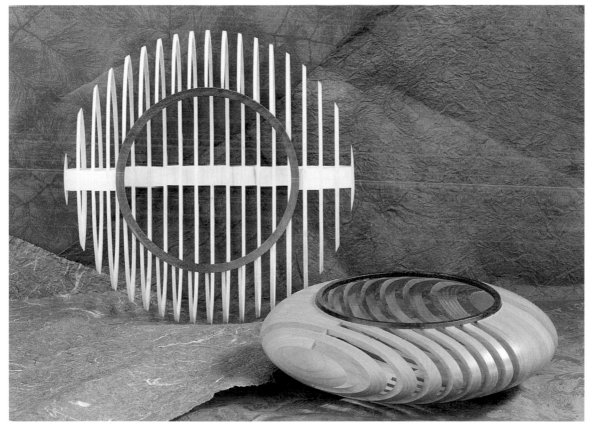

Left: Moiré in Maple and Padauk, maple and padauk, 4" H x 10" DIA

Right: Moiré Hope, maple (bleached) and padauk, 4" H x 12" DIA

Natural Palm,
palm (bleached),
7½" H x 9½" DIA

Turned Palm Wood Bowls by Dewey Garrett

Palms are not usually considered a woodworking material. Indeed, the structural properties of the wood aren't suitable for furniture or construction purposes—the dry wood is a weak, soft material veined with long, tough fibers. However, I've salvaged some cutoffs from tree removal crews and found the wood to be a source for making unique turned art objects.

I am amazed at the composition of palm wood. Unlike conventional woods, no ring structure is present. Instead, the heart of the wood is composed of a wet, pithy material that surrounds an array of randomly placed longitudinal fibers. These fibers or veins are about 0.03 to 0.05 inch in diameter. The density of the veins increases radially—the veins may be separated by 0.3 to 0.4 inches near the center and are almost touching at the bark edge. The bark composition varies with the height of the tree, but generally is composed of several persistent dead leaves. Overall, the bark can be from ¾" to 1½" thick. The fibers are brown in color, while the pithy material is mostly light yellow but may have areas colored in pinks, reds, browns and tans.

One concern when working with this type of wood is how to chuck it for turning. The material's soft, spongy nature does not lend itself to chucking with expanding or contracting jaw chucks, and gluing the soft wet material appears to be a problem. I cut several blocks on the band saw into rounds having diameters of 8" to 15" and heights of 5" to 10". Then I glue these pieces to a scrap wood block mounted on a 4"-diameter faceplate. I use a cyanoacrylate glue and accelerator. I mount the blocks in a conventional manner for faceplate turning with the grain (fibers) perpendicular to the turning axis. The theory here is that adhesives will work best long-grain to long-grain, as in conventional joinery.

Turning the bowls involves conventional techniques. As in most turning where the grain is oriented across the axis, there is a tendency to tear out on the end grain. The only solution to this problem is sharp tools and careful technique, because there isn't much potential to improve a bad surface with sanding. I use a bowl gouge for all exterior and most interior cutting. When the bowl shape has an undercut rim that makes it impossible to use a gouge, I use homemade scrapers with ¼"-square high-speed steel cutters. Some of the bowls I've made incorporate the bark, which is a little tricky to cut through because of its layered and fibrous character. However, on the positive side, the bark does stay attached to the wood instead of separating as often occurs with deciduous woods.

The nature of the material has a particular influence on the design and structure of turned vessels. The size, shape, and wall thickness must be chosen to give a form that is harmonious with the properties of the material. Making very thin bowls isn't practical because they just have no strength when dry. I like a thickness of about ½" for bowls that are 10" to 12" in diameter. The fibers give the finished material an interesting texture when it dries because the pithy material tends to contract relative to the fibers. This contraction makes the fibers protrude slightly, enhancing the texture and feel of the vessel.

After turning and parting off from the wooden faceplate, the finished bowls must be allowed to dry. While cracking and shrinking are unlikely, a new problem I've experienced is the growth of discoloring fungi similar to bread mold. When this occurs, I use strong wood bleaches to kill the fungus and give an entirely new look to the bowls. The bleached woods have a pale, off-white color that is an interesting contrast to the pinks, browns and yellows of a natural bowl. I've finished some bowls with a clear lacquer spray, but I prefer to add no finish. The natural texture and surface are attractive and appropriate for decorative vessels that won't be handled much.

After making numerous cross-grain bowls and gaining some confidence in the strength of the glue joints and the turning characteristics, I tried some bowls with the grain oriented along the turning axis. Having found no alternate method, I cut and glue blanks mounted on the end grain, again using the modern cyanoacrylate adhesive. The turning of the exterior of these bowls is actually easier than the cross-grain bowls, since the end-grain mounting makes the cuts go with the grain as in conventional spindle turning. Again, the cutting and final shaping must be carefully made since sanding cannot fix any problems made in cutting. The interior of the end-grain bowls can be hogged out with gouges or small-tipped scrapers. The final cuts must be made carefully with sharp tools.

The end-grain bowls are a real delight to make and open up new possibilities in design and texture. Tall vessels accentuate the visibility of the fiber structure.

Giles Gilson

Giles Gilson is a man of varied interests and drives. As a child he was fascinated with the technical aspects of cars and airplanes. As soon as he could, he began drawing schematics of motors and designing new body forms that pleased his eye—a lifelong pursuit. In 1991 he built the body for a racing car sponsored by Honda of America. Today, he designs, builds and flies radio-controlled aircraft. Giles is also known to build his own machines to help produce his sculptures.

Giles spent a good deal of time in theater and stage production, working with an accomplished director who wouldn't accept mediocrity in any form. He says he has incorporated this attitude into whatever he does. He is a jazz musician and he enjoys traveling and experiencing new cultures.

"I think all of these different things come together and are expressed in my work," says Giles, noting that he could probably fill volumes trying to explain the whole process.

He says he is often surprised with the final outcome of a piece. "There are many pieces that I'd love to keep if I could afford it," laments Giles. "But Mr. Bill Collector is dangerous when he's not happy. Besides, if you don't sell the piece, you'll stagnate. I like the feeling I get when the pieces are selling because I feel motivated to create more. When you have all the pieces around you, they clutter up your space. You just look at them and don't feel a need to make any more."

For Giles, his work is a means to understanding himself and humanity. "I suppose I am focused primarily on philosophy," he says. "When you spend so much time studying technical material, it naturally leads you to philosophical thoughts. I'm going toward learning what people are all about. I learn more about myself. My favorite answer is 'I just don't know—but I'm finding out.'"

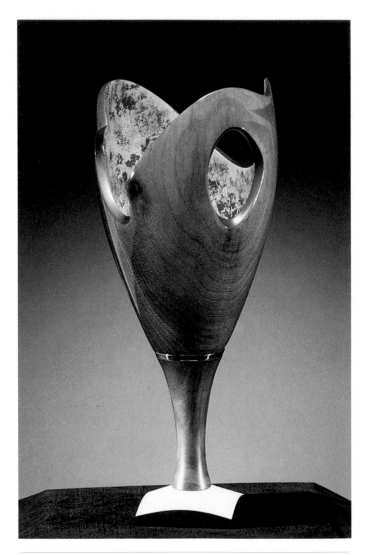

Imagine, lacquered walnut, sculpted open-form ribbon, yellow, red and blue interior, brass ring, walnut foot, Corian base, 11½" H x 4¾" DIA

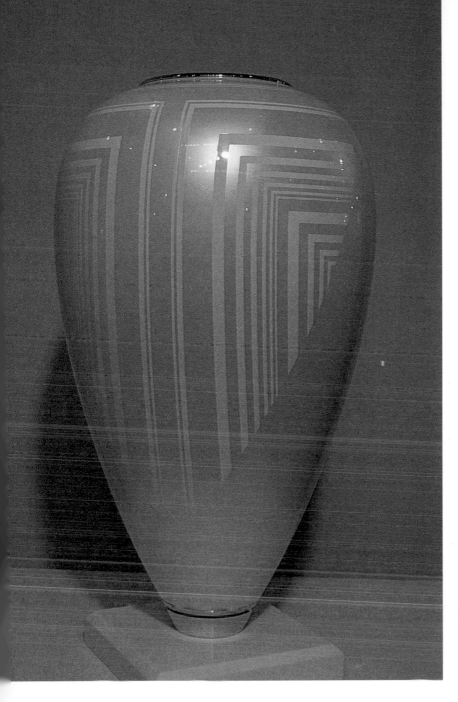

White on White Graphic Vase, lacquered basswood, aluminum, 20" H x 12" DIA

Ribbon Globe, padauk base, 7½" H x 6" DIA

119

Robyn Horn

From her studio in Little Rock, Arkansas, Robyn Horn creates turned-wood sculptures resembling geodes, which are stones found in areas such as Mexico and Brazil. Richard Long, the British ephemeral artist, stated that he loved to work with stone because it is what makes up the earth. Robyn feels she may be a frustrated stone carver, being irresistibly drawn to objects made of stone—goedes, gemstones, monoliths and millstones. "The process of the wood materializing into these stone shapes is the basis of what I am trying to accomplish creatively," says Robyn. "Artists are definitely influenced by the nature of the material and its resistance to being changed. Changing the wood, changing the conception of its form is the intriguing part of creating for me. The look and feel of wood lends itself to a warmer feeling than stone, which adds to the intrinsic value of this material."

Robyn's work has been represented in numerous exhibits throughout the United States, including the Year of the Craft—White House Collection in 1993 and, for the last five years, at the del Mano Gallery in Los Angeles, California.

photo by Bill Parsons

Natural-Edge Geode, chittam, 6" H x 8" W

120

Split Geode,
box elder burl,
ebony and maple,
14" W
"The turned wood
sculptures I make
resemble geodes
which are stones
found in areas such
as Mexico and
Brazil. Inside the
stones is a hollow
cavity where
projecting quartz
crystals form from
mineral deposits
that seep into the
stones. These
crystals create a
sharp contrast to the
rough exterior."

photo by Bill Parsons

Stepping Stone, cocobolo,
16" H x 14" W
"As my work evolves, I
have focused increasingly
on the surface, leaving
thick substantial walls that
can accommodate the
movement and still be
aesthetically pleasing to
the touch as well as to the
viewer."

photo by Bill Parsons

121

Michael Hosaluk

AK photo by Grant Kernan

Michael Hosaluk is a craftsman, artist, designer, innovator and educator who lives outside Saskatoon, Saskatchewan, with his wife, Marilyn, and four children. Growing up on a farm with no modern conveniences, handwork was a way of life."I remember the toys my father made, the clothes my mother made, the strong ethnic influence from my grandmother," says Michael. "My brother and I were always making things. So it's no surprise that handwork would become my way of life."

An internationally recognized woodturner, Michael has lectured and demonstrated extensively throughout Canada, the United States and Australia. In 1993, he was invited to teach in New Zealand. His works have been exhibited throughout the world, including The Royal Ontario Museum in Toronto, The Woodturning Center in Philadelphia and The Saskatchewan Arts Board, where his pieces have been placed in permanent collections.

Michael predominantly uses wood from Saskatchewan, procuring it from abandoned logging sites, private tree cutters, garbage sites and salvage yards. "What I find here is as exotic as any species in the world. The process of finding the material, cutting it, then seeing the finished product has given me a greater reverence for materials and my work."

Michael is comfortable using any media that serves his purpose. His work covers a wide range of objects and materials, ranging from functional vessels and furniture to entirely sculptural pieces. "I am constantly challenging the limits of interpretation in the field of woodturning," he says. "As a result, my work displays a strong command of material used to explore exciting ideas."

He describes his current work as 20th-Century Primitive, weaving stories from his travels and life experiences. "No longer is the material the prime focus, but a starting point to express myself," he says. "My work possesses character and gesture, color and texture. It is humorous and elegant, very contemporary and full of references to architecture, nature and culture."

Michael remains active in his community, freely sharing with others what he has learned. "The growth of a community has always been important to me," he says. "To see craft progress the way it has, and to know that you have been a part of this progression, helps to make my life richer and nurture my growth as a craftsperson. We are all in this together."

Fish Bowl—
"Wood with splits, cracks, or nondescript grain become a starting point of design. It's our ideas that are important."

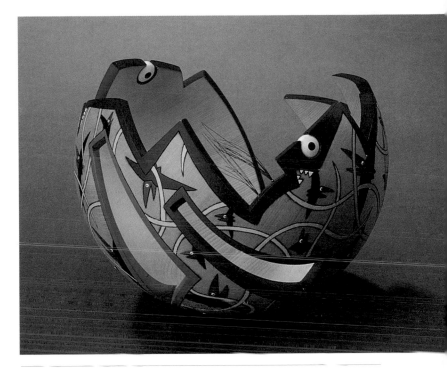

Waterfall

Bird Bowl

Incised Bowl—
"Craft goes beyond the
pleasure of our senses
and deals not only with
aesthetics, but with our
social and ideological
lives."

Jim Hume

For as long as he can remember, Jim Hume has been making things of wood, metal, or "whatever." After graduating from high school, he spent 10 years working in furniture and cabinet shops, and for the last 24 years, has made his living as a custom race car fabricator, doing woodworking and model building as time permitted. In 1989, using his antique 1928 Logan machine lathe, woodturning captured his imagination and has held it ever since.

"I consider myself a dimensional artist but have no idea where my creative/artistic drive comes from," says Jim. "When I do ponder the question, I find my mind has wandered back to the workbench. I am, plain and simple, a man who enjoys creating interesting and imaginative things. My satisfaction comes from taxing my abilities to the fullest by designing unique and complex pieces."

The functional beauty of classical vessels has always captured Jim's imagination, and he relishes the challenge of reproducing these timeless forms in wood. "The segmented construction enables me to control visual texture, while carving introduces alternative surface textures and allows sculptural shapes unattainable on the lathe," he says. "I also use nesting techniques, which allow portions of one section to overlay onto another. Combining these methods has opened entirely new avenues of design possibilities." In the December 1994 and the March 1995 issues of *American Woodturner*, featured articles, "Segmented Urns" and "Close Tolerance Nesting," elaborate on the techniques Jim uses.

Jim is a founding member of Artwood, a co-operative woodworking gallery in Historic Fairhaven-Bellingham, Washington. His work has been featured in numerous shows, galleries and publications.

Number Fifty-Seven, maple, walnut and quilted maple

Number Fifty-Two, walnut, holly, African wenge, maple burl, cherry and mahogany

Number Sixty, padauk, holly, yellow cedar and mahogany

C. R. "Skip" Johnson

You need only glance at the letterhead which reads, "C. R. 'Skip' Johnson, Wisconsin's Wonderfully Wild Woodworking Wizard and All Around Good Guy," to understand the whimsy in the woodworking of this artist.

When asked about the creation of the Trump-a-kazoo, the Sax-a-kazoo and the Clarinet-a-kazoo, Skip enlightened us with his four-step process, "Need—a second bathroom; Action—a woodworker turned plumber's helper; Influences—pipes, faucets, elbows and kazoos; Results —'The Plumber's Kazoo Band.'"

Skip was born in Painted Post, New York, and received a Bachelor of Science degree from the State University of New York-Oswego. After receiving his MFA from the School for American Craftsmen, he started his teaching career.

Retiring after 25 years at the University of Wisconsin-Madison, Skip holds the title of Professor Emeritus of Art. Over a span of four decades, he has presented numerous lectures and workshops and his work has been included in countless exhibitions, collections and publications.

Sax-a-kazoo, walnut and maple with metal kazoo inside, 21" H x 8" x 8"

Trump-a-kazoo, cherry with metal kazoo inside, 23" H x 5" x 7"

Clarinet-a-kazoo, walnut and maple with metal kazoo inside, 23" H x 8" x 8"

John Jordan

John Jordan is a woodturner from Antioch (Nashville), Tennessee. Known primarily for his textured and carved hollow vessels, John has been featured in nearly every major turning exhibition over the past five years, including "International Lathe-Turned Objects-Challenge V," and "Redefining the Lathe-Turned Object III." His work has received numerous awards, and is in the permanent collections of several museums and corporations, including the Renwick Gallery of the Smithsonian, the High Museum of Art in Atlanta, the American Craft Museum in New York City, and the White House in Washington, D.C.

John is in great demand as a demonstrator/teacher, traveling extensively teaching at universities, craft schools, turning groups and trade shows throughout the United States, Canada, and the United Kingdom, including an annual week at world-famous Arrowmont School of Arts and Crafts. His work is frequently seen in publications in several countries as are articles he has written. He has also produced two woodturning videos, which have received very favorable reviews.

John's pieces are initially turned on the lathe, from fresh, green logs, using a number of techniques and tools that have evolved over the years. Each piece is then hand-carved and textured, using a variety of different hand and small power tools. This texturing process is very labor intensive, and can take as much as several days to complete. There is little room for error in this carving—one small slip can ruin the piece. A light lacquer finish is applied to most pieces, including the dyed work.

"The pieces I make are simple but finely detailed vessels," he says. "Manipulating the color and patterns in the wood to complement the form, and the texturing and carving to create visual and tactile contrasts, are important parts of the process and the result. I feel that what is most important is the intangible quality about the piece being "right" that comes with putting emotion and feeling into the work.

"Many of the woods that I use are from the dump or construction sites. I find great satisfaction in creating objects from material that was otherwise destined to be buried or burned."

Black Textured Jar, turned, carved and dyed maple, 12" H x 8" DIA (Neil Kaye collection)

Black Textured Vessels, turned, carved and dyed maple,
tallest is 12" H (collection of David and Ruth Waterbury)

Bonnie Klein

Bonnie Klein is a full-time woodturner in the Northwest, specializing in smaller-scale turnings, such as spin tops, pens, earrings and lidded containers. Her father was a home builder, and Bonnie spent many days at his job sites, hammering and sawing away at scrap lumber.

"I would love to have taken woodshop in high school, but girls weren't allowed," she says. Her love of woodworking was rekindled about 20 years ago when her daughter wanted a dollhouse. During the process of building, lighting and furnishing, she became mostly interested in the tools. This interest led her to design and produce a small woodturning lathe.

The Klein lathe has a 5" swing and is 12" between centers. A wide range of accessories is available, including chucks, tools, a threading jig and an indexing plate. This was a new beginning for what Bonnie calls "small-scale turning" and what has developed into an area of its own in the woodturning world, with tools, classes, projects and even gallery shows. With a small lathe comes the opportunity to be more portable, allowing it to travel to crafts fairs or even on vacation.

Bonnie turns for the love of the creative process. "I am addicted to discovery, progress and the fact that perfection is forever elusive, but, as I strive for it, yesterday's challenges become the basic skills of tomorrow," she says. Because of her love for woodturning, she has been invited to demonstrate and give workshops in Australia, England, Ireland and Canada, as well as all over the United States. "I love the teaching and demonstrating, but I have also attended just about every woodturning event that has happened recently." Describing herself as a "perpetual student," Bonnie knows there is always more to learn.

She was elected to the board of The American Association of Woodturners six years ago, serving as vice president for the last five years. She loves teaching young people and volunteers many hours sharing woodturning with Girl Scouts, Cub Scouts and school shop classes.

Spin Tops, various woods with chatter work and finished with colored pens, 2" DIA

Bone Box, ebony insert, 1½" DIA
"I love the distinct smell of the various woods, the sound of the shavings as they are cut by a sharp tool, and how quickly a form appears from a block of material. Experimenting with turning unusual materials such as bone, plastic, tagua nuts, aluminum and horn has led to many more interesting sensations for the eyes, ears, hands, and nose."

Box with Threaded Lid, spalted maple, 2¼" DIA

Bud Latven

After serving in the army in the late 1960s, Bud Latven traveled west and settled in New Mexico in 1972. He worked in a production cabinet shop and started his own furniture business in 1973, making Southwest-style furniture. In 1974, Bud began working with slabbed burlwoods from the Pacific Northwest, making mostly table configurations and marketing this work in galleries in Santa Fe and at crafts shows in the Southwest. In the early 1980s, he took two years off to build a home in 4th of July Canyon, the only place in New Mexico where there are large stands of maple trees.

In 1982, Bud started woodturning as a fluke when he got a small job doing some production goblets. In 1984, he co-wrote an article with Addie Draper on "Segmented Woodturning" for *Fine Woodworking* magazine, which launched his career in the woodturning field. He participated in gallery exhibitions and national crafts shows through the 1980s, while developing his own particular style in constructive woodturning. His work has evolved through various approaches from shoe-polished Indian pot forms to metalized and airbrushed vessel forms. He is most recognized for his segmented hardwood constructions, such as "Prairie Island" which is featured on the cover of this book.

Bud's work is held in public and private collections throughout the country. He is currently represented by Connell Gallery in Atlanta, Georgia.

Hyperboloid, American fiddleback maple, African ebony and avonite, 16" H x 12" DIA

Atsinna, Australian lacewood, African ebony and avonite, 16" H x 5½" DIA (Fleur Bresler private collection)

Hugh McKay

Born in 1951, Hugh McKay has been a craftsman-designer all of his adult life, primarily working with wood but also metal and stone. After college, he felt a strong desire to work with his hands and took a job in a woodturning shop. After turning there for several years, Hugh became interested in all aspects of fine woodworking, studying any materials he could find. In order to keep up with his interests, he started his own shop in 1979. "I fully intended to earn a living making furniture, but since the late 1980s, I have found myself totally absorbed in the possibilities of expression in woodturning," he says. Living in Gold Beach, Oregon, provides him with a constant source of domestic burls, which he uses in his woodturning.

With his strong foundational skills in woodturning, Hugh started experimenting with the tooling and techniques that could enable him to turn almost any hollowed-vase form in wood on the lathe. His desire was to have the same freedom of shape as a potter has on the potter's wheel. When you look at his turnings, you can see that he has accomplished this goal.

Hugh also carves, sandblasts and inlays various materials on the outside of the hollowed-wood form. He is constantly investigating and developing new techniques and materials for this purpose. "The 'senseless adornment' of an idea (the turned hollowed-wood vessel in this case) that was once considered practical and utilitarian has always fascinated me as a craftsman," he says. "The irrational or 'wild' elements found in nature are the design basis I prefer to use for adorning my turned-wood forms. Though I may use designs suggested by nature, I am not concerned with expressing 'naturalness.' Rather, I view each new work as an opportunity to experiment with the chaotic character I see in much of nature. This 'chaos' represents a higher order to me, which I am attempting to better understand through my work. Marrying this 'chaos' to the mundane rigid symmetry of the turned-wood form also lets me deal with another fascination of mine, bringing together the dissimilar to make a new creation."

Tripot #3, maple burl, 9" H x 24" x 24"
"This piece consists of three turned vase forms from one piece of wood. They are multiple axis turnings with no glue joints. The natural edge of the burl forms the handles."

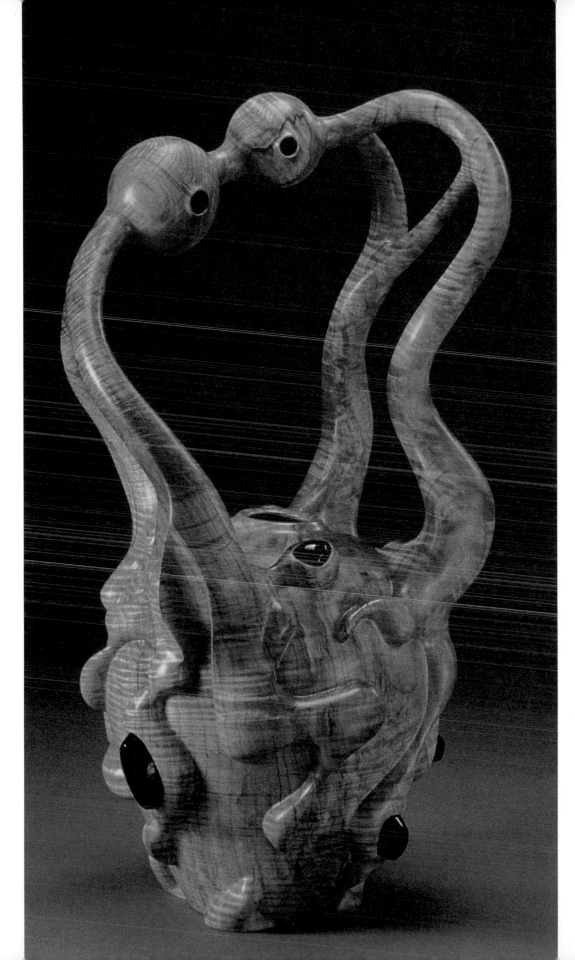

Yes, fiddleback maple and soapstone, 24" H x 13" x 13"
"This piece is only partially sanded with coarse-grit paper. There are odd-shaped holes in the main vase form which are inlaid with black soapstone. The two round forms at the top of the piece are hollowed out on the lathe, the whole piece being turned on the lathe."

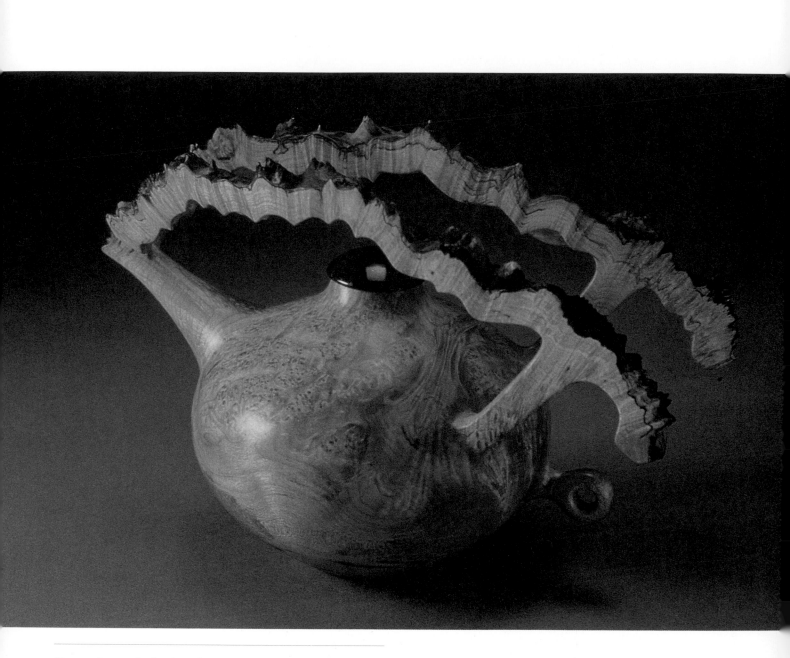

T-pot #8, maple burl and soapstone, 9" H x 12" x 7"
"This piece is also a multiple-axis turning as the vessel
and the spout are turned out on the lathe. It is made
from one piece of wood using the natural edge of the
burl for its handles."

Johannes Michelsen

Johannes Michelsen was born in the city of Copenhagen, in Denmark, and moved to the United States when he was four years old. Although he started at age 10, Johannes spent the next 20 years turning only on an occasional basis. In 1977, he began to pursue the turned vessel as an art form. His efforts were simple one-piece footed and natural-edged bowls of burl or spalted wood of local origin. His work progressed from these simple one-piece turnings into more complicated vases constructed of many elements with a variety of finishes.

For years, Johannes had tossed around the idea of turning headwear, but life, being what it is, left him little time to develop the idea. Then in 1990 he was invited to a fellow woodturner's wedding. Since the wedding had a country-western theme, Johannes knew this was the perfect time to try out his wooden hats. The cherry-wood Stetson that he wore to the wedding drew so much attention that it launched his "sawmillinery" business.

From his studio in Manchester Center, Vermont, Johannes has made over 500 hats. His hats are not only sculptural, but are custom-fitted. Each hat weighs between 6 to 9 ounces, no more than common hats. Due to their unique magnetism, they are being sought after by collectors and noncollectors alike.

"To get a custom fit, I measure the head with a lead-filled 'Curvex' ruler, and transfer the shape to paper. Measuring front to back and side to side, I come up with an average for the hat size. To this I add a sufficient amount to compensate for shrinkage, and then turn the resulting diameter. I form the hats from a native northern hardwood— maple, ash, butternut, walnut, or yellow birch—to a final thickness of about ³⁄₃₂" and slightly thicker at the edge of the brim and the band for strength."

Stephen Mines

Stephen Mines was born in Muskegon, Michigan. After attending Michigan State University, he made the move to California, where he studied at the Pasadena Playhouse College of Theatre Arts and the Choinard Art Institute. His philosophy on education is, "No degrees . . . no regrets!" Stephen now lives with his wife, Shirley, in Panorama City, California, working lathe magic from his backyard shop.

For years Stephen was an actor, who dreamed of someday building yachts. Instead, a master furniture maker saw his woodworking talent and encouraged him to pursue it. For 17 years, Stephen operated a furniture manufacturing business which specialized in French and American reproductions. However, he was not comfortable with his large business, and returned to a more rewarding, single-person woodworking style. Today he specializes in custom, ornamental spindle turning, using exotic woods and his own unique designs. The need for artistic woodturning brought Stephen to create his magic wands, two of which are featured here. The wands are held in the private collection of Irving Lipton of Los Angeles, California.

Stephen's wands have won various awards. His most recently published work includes the March 1994 issue of *American Woodturner* magazine. His work was shown in the juried exhibition, Challenge V: International Lathe-Turned Objects. He has produced a new video, *Hydraulic Tracing/Ornamental Turning*, in which he shares his expertise and experience with other woodturners. Stephen enjoys living happily and making "it" happen now.

Crystal Wand #3, 2" solid acrylic rod with natural quartz crystal point, 2" DIA x 43½" L (Irving Lipton private collection)

Magic Wand #140, padauk with straight pierced flutes at the top, left and right, spirals (checkering effect) at the handle, seven tapered spiral leads for the shaft, malachite cabachons and a quartz crystal point, 1.8125" DIA x 42¾" L (Irving Lipton private collection)
"This was a basic exercise in applying various ornamentation to a spindle. The addition of the cabachons and the crystal seemed to make it 'feel right' and completed."

Philip Moulthrop

Philip Moulthrop was born in 1947 in Atlanta, Georgia. He received his Bachelor of Arts degree from West Georgia College and a Juris Doctorate from Woodrow Wilson College of Law.

However, at 32 years of age, Philip was ready to follow in the footsteps of his father, Ed. The elder Moulthrop taught the craft to his son on a lathe which Philip had made himself. "In addition to my self-made lathe, I black-smith all of my tools using a forge and anvil," he says. "These tools are designed specifically to perform hollow-bowl turning using my own equipment."

The turned wooden bowls and vases by Philip are created from green sections of native southeastern trees. The green log is first roughed into the initial shape and then treated to prevent cracking. The piece is then dried and re-turned on the lathe to its final form. After numerous sandings, the piece is coated with several coats of finish.

The featured bowl is 8¼" high by 9¾" diameter and made from ash leaf maple, which was turned at a 90-degree angle to the growth position. This allows the center patterns to appear on opposite sides. This wood is commonly known as box elder and is found throughout much of the United States.

Bowl, ash leaf maple (commonly known as box elder), 8¼" H x 9¾" DIA

Rude Osolnik

Portrait by Kay Browning

At 80 years young, Rude Osolnik is still turning out wood masterpieces. He is held in high esteem by his peers, setting the standards for woodturners around the world.

For many years, Rude was an instructor in the Industrial Arts Department at Berea College in Berea, Kentucky, later becoming chairman of that department. He has taught workshops and demonstrated woodturning throughout the United States for more than 40 years. In 1990, Rude taught a major workshop in New Zealand.

His countless awards, publications and exhibitions span five decades. In 1992, he received Kentucky's Governor's Award for Lifetime Achievement in the Arts. His work is included in a European tour, entitled "Out of the Woods: Turned Wood by American Craftsmen," as a cultural presentation of the United States which runs through 1997.

Laminated Birch, 3¼" H x 6" DIA

Lilac Burl, 7½" H x 8" DIA

142

William Schmidt

Born in 1945, William Schmidt began his woodturning career in 1971, in Berkley, California, while trying to "resolve matters with the Ohio draft board." Inspired by Bay Area woodturner Bruce Robbins, Bill began turning crochet hooks and other small functional items. He avoided significant contact with other turners for several years, while developing his own style and turning methodology. Utilizing concepts from his college engineering training and machine-shop experience, he maintains a strictly freehand, no-repetition approach, while producing volume production turnings.

It took nearly a year to develop his cutting methods, and the design was refined over several years to what it is today. After 24 years of turning professionally, he is still discovering new methods and refinements.

A toolmaker at heart, Bill prefers making functional items that the everyday person can afford and can use comfortably. "Art should be an integral part of everyday life—affordable and usable," he says. Seeing the small, exotic woodturnings as similar to jewelry, he attempts to maintain jewelrylike quality throughout.

Most ideas for items come from customer requests, and a great many of Bill's items are tools for textile work, such as crocheting, knitting and lacemaking. "My most original idea is the baby rattle, and that originated from a friend's comment," Bill says. "The goal is to take a concept, then develop the item functionally and/or aesthetically to be significantly different (preferably unrecognizably so) from the source of inspiration."

Annoyed by the art world's disdain for "little sticks," and a desire to master broader areas of woodturning, Bill began turning bowls in 1978. Restricting himself to wood destined for firewood piles or trash heaps, he considers it a high challenge of craftsmanship to turn "future firewood" into quality pieces of functional and decorative art. Bill also produces turned wall mirrors up to a yard across. All larger pieces are of domestic hardwoods. "I restrict my use of exotics to pen-size and smaller items," he says.

Returning to Mansfield, Ohio, in 1973, Bill teamed up in 1976 with Diana Andra, who makes tatting shuttles and does some woodturning. Bill and Diana display and sell their work at crafts shows from Chicago to Maryland and in select crafts shops and galleries nationwide, under the name, Turn of the Century.

Spalted Beech Bowl, 14" DIA
"We produce our work for the everyday Joe or Jane—members of the general public who are not rich, yet who want, and well deserve, to be able to purchase fine artistic items within their budget."

143

Rattles and Crochet Hooks

Eugene Sexton

Eugene Sexton was born in West Virginia and reared in Ohio. After serving a tour in the army, he settled back in Ohio and began working on the assembly line at General Motors. As a hobbyist in the woodturning field, he was plagued by the same common dilemma as other woodturners—bad wood. This came in the form of wood stock that was blue-stained or checked or otherwise extremely hard to work with. With these and other problems in mind, Gene resolved himself to find a better wood.

With financial and moral support from his wife, he resigned from his job and started experimenting with various methods and processes that would allow for an alteration of the wood composition without relinquishing any of the better traits of the species. Without the hindrance of a formal education in the field of forestry, he was able to pursue avenues of research that were not previously explored.

Now after approximately 19 years of trial and error, he has developed a process called ESP-90 that has accomplished the task after which he set out. In fact, the wood is even better than anticipated. Blue stain can be controlled and/or eliminated. Checking and splitting has been minimized or eliminated. Insects that would normally attack the wood do not, and biodeterioration has been stopped. This process is post-harvest, and the treated wood can be stored in log form until needed. The ESP-90 process does not require chemicals, kiln drying or any other conventional methods of drying. The cost is approximately $2 per tree, without regard to size or species.

In 1994, Gene sold rights to the process to ES TECH, Inc. for an undisclosed sum and stock in the company. He also moved to Georgia and became vice president of research for the firm. With this corporate backing, he has improved the wood processes and expanded his research into the plant and seed field. Variations of the original process allow the company to treat seeds or seedlings, and the resultant plant has a faster, more vigorous growth and higher crop yield than the non-treated. The same applies to tree seeds and seedlings. This variation provides for higher yield from the forests and the preservation of indigenous species. Also, the company is able to store treated nuts and produce for an extended period of time without cold storage.

ES TECH has received numerous offers to purchase ESP-90 from major corporations in the wood, chemical and seed industries, and they are being considered. However, in concurrence with Gene's wish that ESP-90 become an item of public domain, ES TECH is pursuing the U.S. Government to purchase ESP-90 for resale and distribution to the private sector.

Page 146: Large pedestal made of wood, which is a product of the ESP-90 process.

Robert Sonday

Born in 1953 in Jefferson, Iowa, Robert Sonday taught himself the techniques of furniture making and woodturning. What began as an apprenticeship in construction developed into a custom cabinet-making business. Today, however, Robert produces two distinct woodturning products—chairs and bowls.

"I have always been attracted to revolving things and to creation by subtraction," says Robert, who works out of his workshop-home in Free Union, Virginia. "The act of turning is so satisfying. I can put a chosen chunk of a tree on the lathe, and, in one day, I can turn and finish a new study of shape as it relates to material, use, and meaning."

Robert's bowls are simple, elegant and graceful and have been featured in exhibitions across the country, including "Challenge V: International Lathe-Turned Objects" and "Art from the Lathe" at the Hagley Museum in Wilmington, Delaware.

"I love the peaceful rhythm of shavings coming off continuously in a good clean cut, but I always have to be ready for that piece to explode when I've gone a bit too far," he says. "It's a challenge that's a delight to my temperament."

Myrtle #4, myrtle, 9" H x 7" DIA
"I turn the myrtle wood to the desired shape, beading the exterior surface and rounding the bowl edges delicately."

Djembe, silver beech, 24" H x 13½" DIA

Alan Stirt

Alan Stirt was born in Brooklyn, New York, in 1946. After graduating from Harpur College in l969 with a BA in psychology, he wasn't sure what he wanted to do. He turned down a graduate fellowship at the University of Illinois, worked at various jobs, and traveled for a year.

In 1970 he started doing some wood carving and fell in love with the material. A book about woodturning, found in a local crafts store, revealed that the lathe could be a kind of carving tool. He spent some time, "with a book in one hand and a turning tool in the other," and taught himself how to turn.

Bowl and platter forms have been Alan's main preoccupation since 1972. "Bowls, whether of wood, clay, glass or metal, have always meant more for the cultures which produce them than just utilitarian purpose," says Alan. "Even bowls which were, and are, used every day have been made and acquired with an obvious concern for aesthetics.

"As a contemporary bowl maker, I am aware of being part of a long history of bowl makers throughout the world. My primary goal has always been to make objects that feel like they belong. Whether a utilitarian salad bowl or a piece meant just be be touched or looked at, I want each piece to have a sense of rightness. I hope that the sense of satisfaction in making a good piece can be somehow transferred to someone viewing and holding one of my pieces."

Alan is an internationally recognized woodturner who has traveled throughout the United States, as well as England, Ireland, New Zealand and Canada, giving workshops in the art and craft of woodturning. His work is represented in many public and private collections that include the American Craft Museum in New York, the High Museum of Art in Atlanta and the White House Permanent Craft Collection.

Spring Rhythm, maple burl turned and carved, 16½" DIA "This pattern was created with a curved template on the piece after I had indexed it with a protractor. I cut the groove with the electric gouge and used an abrasive flap wheel to round the edges."

149

Tidal Rip, cherry wood dyed with milk paint and carved, 19½" DIA

150

Bob Stocksdale

For more than 50 years, Bob Stocksdale has been turning his decorative wooden bowls, a skill he acquired while serving in federal detention camps during World War II. Stating that "war never solves anything," Bob was considered a Conscientious Objector, and served four years at three different camps. It was at one of these camps that Helen Winnemore, owner of a gallery in Columbus, Ohio, discovered Bob's unique and elegant style and started exhibiting his pieces. Winnemore's words of wisdom that "quality is everything" have stayed with Bob through the years and are evident in every bowl he creates.

Although well known for his remarkable repertoire of exotic wood, Bob's concern lies mainly with the aesthetics of his finished product, concentrating on the grain and color of the wood. Never having a preconceived idea of what a piece will look like, he leaves it entirely up to the wood, designing while turning on the lathe.

He does almost all his turning with a single ½" gouge. "The fewer tools I have, the less time spent sharpening and switching them," he says. "If I can do it all with one tool, why not? It seems to work out quite well." Indeed it has, as he is referred to by his peers as "the finest woodturner in America."

Bob is married to Kay Sekimachi, a world-renowned fiber artist, and they often exhibit together, combining two different art forms in perfect harmony. Their pieces have been shown in museums and galleries around the world.

Flowering Pear,
3½" x 6" DIA

Lignum Vitae, 6½" x 7" DIA

Frank Sudol

Frank Sudol got started in woodworking as a part-time carpenter and furniture maker, specializing in rocking chairs. For 20 years he dabbled in turning, but has only been concentrating on serious turning since his retirement after 17 years of teaching. After taking numerous workshops from some of the most prominent turners in the world, Frank had reached the level of skill where he was able to create his own niche in the turning world. In 1993, he attended his first AAW conference in New York and exhibited the thin-walled, pierced work that he is known for today. His work was featured on the cover of the June 1994 issue of the British *Woodturning Journal* and has been seen in other publications around the world.

"Almost all of my work is made from local paper birch. It is turned green to at least $\frac{1}{16}$" thickness but is best at $\frac{1}{20}$". When dry, I pierce the walls with a dental drill," he says. "The air-driven dental drill is used because of its ability to spin at 350,000 rpm as opposed to the 35,000 rpm of the electric units. The high speed prevents grabbing and cuts more rapidly. The patterns are freehand drawings that show the delicacy of and respect for nature around us. My biology background shows through as I tend to feature the fragile earth and nature itself in unique ways on my turned vessels."

At 61, Frank spends an increasing amount of time demonstrating and teaching woodturning. "To date, my highest honors were the invitations to demonstrate my pierced work at the 1994 AAW Symposium in Colorado and the 1995 AAW Symposium in California," he says. "I was also thrilled to teach at Dale Nish's seminar in Provo, Utah, in 1995." Since then, the opportunities keep coming to travel and teach throughout the United States and Canada.

Dragon Fly Vase, birch, 21" H

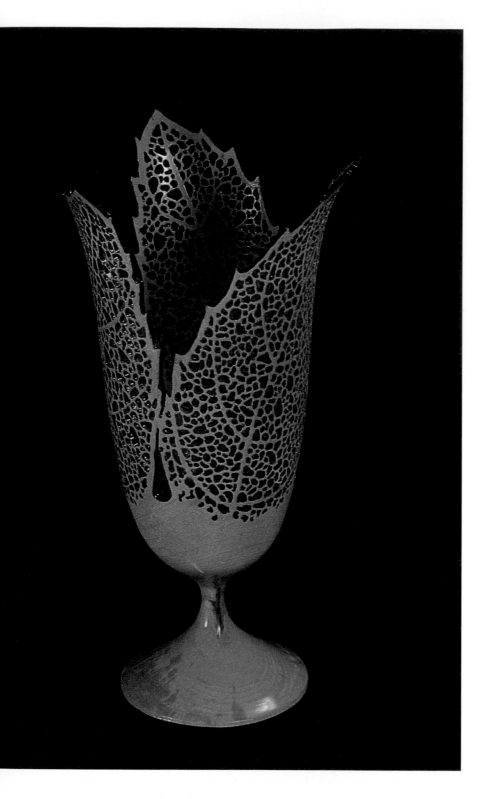

Chalice, birch, 7" H

Airy Spaces, birch body and lid on mahogany base, 20" H

Hans Weissflog

Hans Joachim Weissflog was born in Hönnersum, Germany, in 1954. After studying mechanical engineering for two years, he entered the Hildesheim Holzminden College in the field of design. At that same time, he took his apprenticeship in woodturning under Professor Bockelmann.

Hans' miniature boxes are included in museum collections throughout Europe and the United States. In 1993, he was the featured artist at the Del Mano Gallery in Philadelphia, Pennsylvania, and continues to exhibit his work there every year.

Unless you hold one of his boxes in your hand, it's hard to get a feel for the size and workmanship involved. The featured box is turned and broken through from African blackwood and boxwood on a simple lathe. This ball-box measures 2" in diameter.

Ball Box, African blackwood and boxwood, turned broken through, 2" DIA

Page 156: Ball Box open

John Wooller

Although born and raised in England, John Wooller has spent the last 30 years in Australia. As you look at his sculptures, it is hard to believe that his interest in woodturning began less than six years ago. In that time span, he has gone from making bowls as a hobby to producing sculptures as a profession.

John turns to literature as a source of inspiration for his work, finding unlimited visual ideas and intellectual concepts which can readily be turned into tangible form. Most often he chooses a theme, and then goes about producing about a dozen pieces, each one interpreting a different aspect of the theme.

Numerous magazines have featured articles on John's work, which has won awards from competitive woodworking exhibitions around the world. While his sculptures are exhibited widely throughout Australian galleries, his work is also held in private collections worldwide.

John uses jarrah burl almost exclusively as the amorphous structure for his pieces, finding that the richness of its color enhances his work best. Many times he uses the natural edge as contrast to the superimposed orderliness of the turning and carving. Although he does some carving, multiple-axis turning is John's basic technique for removing wood.

His technique for creating Music of the Spheres is very interesting. The slab of jarrah burl was turned on three axes to form the outer shell and its supporting ribs. Turning on three more axes produced the two hollow forms and a set of rings. After reversing the slab on the lathe, the outer shell, two ribs and two hollow forms were completed. Turning on a further axis was necessary to complete the set of interlocking rings. Part of the outer shell and the unwanted part of the internal web were then carved away to leave the hollow forms and the rings suspended inside the shell.

Music of the Spheres, jarrah burl turned and carved, 23⅝" H (Irving Lipton private collection)

And the Daughters of Darkness Flame Like the Fawkes' Fires Still, jarrah burl, 32¼" H (R and T Pearson collection)

A Sea of Troubles, jarrah burl and brass on a granite base, 35¹⁄₁₆" H (University of Canberra, Australia collection)

Acknowledgments

In addition to thanking all of the great artists who generously loaned photos or turnings and provided copy for the projects and gallery sections, I wish to express my sincerest gratitude to many others who have helped along the way. The following have provided suggestions, direction, and ideas that were especially valuable: Patricia Spielman, for design assistance and encouragement; Albert LeCoff, for information about the Turning Center; Rick Mastelli, editor of *American Woodturner*, for his leads; Al Rich, for his demonstrations and helpful tips; Betty Scarpino, for her thoughtful suggestions and time reviewing this book; Bonnie Klein, Bob Chapman, Nick Cook, Hank Bardenhagen, and Gerald Veenendaal for their helpful influence and efforts; and Wally Dickerman, for his centering-jig idea and tips about double-faced tape. A hearty thanks to Jerry Glaser of Glaser Engineering, for technical expertise about new tooling and for his review of this book; Ron and Anne Ashby of Liberon/Star Supplies, for some good finishing ideas; Darrel Nish of Craft Supplies USA, for ideas, leads and photos; and David Kelly of Robert Sorby Tools, for some excellent photos. The great cooperation from Richard Lukes, Clead Christiansen, Delta International Machinery Co., Packard Woodworks, RYOBI, America Corp., Anchor Continental Inc., and the JDS Company is also appreciated.

Special words of praise and thanks are extended to Mark Johnsen of Moonlight Photography, for his patience and valuable assistance. Warm thank-yous to my friends: Dan Kihl, for the southwest designs; Julie Kiehnau, for the typing; and Harvey and Barb Malzahn, my expedient film couriers.

Metric Equivalency Chart

MM-Millimetres   CM-Centimetres

INCHES TO MILLIMETRES AND CENTIMETRES

INCHES	MM	CM	INCHES	CM	INCHES	CM
1/8	3	0.3	9	22.9	30	76.2
1/4	6	0.6	10	25.4	31	78.7
1/2	13	1.3	12	30.5	33	83.8
5/8	16	1.6	13	33.0	34	86.4
3/4	19	1.9	14	35.6	35	88.9
7/8	22	2.2	15	38.1	36	91.4
1	25	2.5	16	40.6	37	94.0
1 1/4	32	3.2	17	43.2	38	96.5
1 1/2	38	3.8	18	45.7	39	99.1
1 3/4	44	4.4	19	48.3	40	101.6
2	51	5.1	20	50.8	41	104.1
2 1/2	64	6.4	21	53.3	42	106.7
3	76	7.6	22	55.9	43	109.2
3 1/2	89	8.9	23	58.4	44	111.8
4	102	10.2	24	61.0	45	114.3
4 1/2	114	11.4	25	63.5	46	116.8
5	127	12.7	26	66.0	47	119.4
6	152	15.2	27	68.6	48	121.9
7	178	17.8	28	71.1	49	124.5
8	203	20.3	29	73.7	50	127.0

Index